Reconciling Man with the Environment

The Leon Sloss Junior
Memorial Lectures in Humanities,
1977

Reconciling Man
with the Environment

ERIC ASHBY , *1904 –*

STANFORD UNIVERSITY PRESS

1978  Stanford, California

Stanford University Press
Stanford, California
© 1978 by the Board of Trustees of the
Leland Stanford Junior University
Printed in the United States of America
ISBN 0-8047-0986-6
LC 77-91909

The Leon Sloss Junior Memorial Lectures are endowed to
support the humanities. It was, therefore, an act of faith on
the part of Stanford University to invite me, a biologist, to
give these lectures, and (I felt) an act of temerity on my part
to accept the invitation. To justify my acceptance I had to
decide what the word "humanities" means to me.

A few years ago Howard Mumford Jones wrote a trench-
ant essay about American humanism. "The Americans," he
wrote, "have substituted something called the humanities
for humanism. Humanism is a philosophy of mankind;
the humanities are simply variant branches ... of expertise"
bringing the same attitude to a speciality whether it is, as
he put it, "metrics of Anglo-Saxon verse or spinal anesthe-
sia." As a scientist, I have a more romantic view of the
humanities than that. It seems to me that the basic difference between science and the humanities is not the choice
of subject; it is the spirit of pursuit (a phrase the philosopher Samuel Alexander used in another context). The
scientific spirit of pursuit is one that tries to eliminate the
human equation, so that the findings will be acceptable to
any rational man anywhere. The humanistic spirit of pursuit is one that does not try to eliminate the human equation; it tries to solve it, and every solution is unique. Every
man converts the oxygen he breathes into carbon dioxide

in the same way. No two men love or act justly or show disdain in the same way, either toward one another or toward nature. These lectures are about the influence of the sentiments upon man's attitude to the environment. I hope this qualifies them to be included in an endowment devoted to the humanities.

My thanks go first of all to Stanford University for honoring me by their invitation, and to the President and some of his colleagues for their hospitality during my stay. In particular I thank my host and hostess, Meredith and Marian Wilson; their home was an idyllic base for a visiting lecturer.

From the Office of Public Events, Vicky Holt and Susan Farr organized the lectures with enviable efficiency; and from Stanford University Press I have had great help and good advice from J. G. Bell and Peter J. Kahn.

For shortcomings in this book I have only myself to blame. But there would have been more of them had it not been for welcome criticisms from some of my friends, especially Mary Anderson, who read the first draft and to whom I am in debt also for preparing the diagrams and the index. Meredith Wilson made a criticism (included in a footnote) that clarifies a difficult point in my argument. Sidney Siskin, of Cornell University, kindly sent me useful material, and I have profited from several criticisms she made of the final draft of the lectures.

Annual Reviews Inc. kindly gave me permission to use two diagrams (Figures 2 and 3) taken from a paper by

Starr, Rudman, and Whipple in the *Annual Review of Energy*.

For the benefit of any scientists who read the book I should explain that the phrase "chain reaction" as I use it is not to suggest an analogy with chain reactions in chemistry; it is used in the figurative sense defined in the *Concise Oxford Dictionary* as "series of events each due to previous ones."

E.A.

Clare College
Cambridge

CONTENTS

ONE

The Chain Reaction

"There is nothing easier than to point out the absence from history books of major phenomena that were imperceptible owing to the slowness of their evolution. They escape the historian's notice because no document expressly mentions them."[1] I quote from Paul Valery, and my theme is an example of his assertion. I believe that man's attitude to nature in Western societies has been changing almost imperceptibly over the last hundred years, and that the change is for the better. This, I realize, is to inject a ray of sunshine through the thunderclouds of environmental doom generated by some distinguished and popular authors; so let me at the outset dispel a possible misunderstanding. I do not underestimate the perils threatening industrial society, though I think that some of the people who warn us about environmental crisis have got their perspectives wrong. Indeed, I think they are wrong to call it a crisis at all. A crisis is a situation that will pass; it can be resolved by temporary hardship, temporary adjustment, technological and political expedients. What we are experiencing is not a crisis: it is a climacteric. For the rest of man's history on earth, so far as one can foretell, he will have to live with problems of population, of resources, of pollution. And the seminal problem remains unsolved: Can man adapt himself to *anticipate* environmental constraints? Or will he (like other animal

3

societies) adapt himself only in *response* to the constraints after they have begun to hurt? In one facet of this problem I see reason for cautious optimism. That is what these lectures are about.

My text, or rather antitext, is a well-worn quotation from Lynn White. "Despite Darwin," he wrote, "we are *not*, in our hearts, part of the natural process. We are superior to nature, contemptuous of it."* This was written only ten years ago. Even if it were true then, it is no longer true. Over protection of the environment there has been a quickening of the public conscience in most industrial countries. There is evidence of a trend in social values from exploitation of nature toward symbiosis with nature. I shall argue that it is a trend to which one can attach that unfashionable word "progress."

Some primitive societies recognize intuitively that man and environment are indivisible. Far from being contemptuous of nature, these societies are in daily and sensitive

* Lynn White Jr., "The Historic Roots of Our Ecologic Crisis," *Science*, 155 (Mar. 1967), p. 1204. The origin of man's possessive attitude to nature is commonly attributed to the Judeo-Christian tradition, reaching back to God's mandate to man to "subdue" the earth, and permeating the Christian tradition with its setting of man apart from other creatures. This assumption has been challenged in an excellent essay by John Passmore (*Man's Responsibility for Nature*, London, 1974), who reminds us that some of the Greeks took a similar view: Aristotle in his *Politics* wrote that "plants are created for the sake of animals, and the animals for the sake of men." Passmore agrees that "Christianity has encouraged man to think of himself as nature's absolute master," but he shows persuasively that it was Bacon and Descartes who set the social values that enjoin men to "effect all things possible" and to "render ourselves the masters and possessors of nature."

and obedient communication with it. Edward Hall, in his delightful book *The Silent Language*,[2] records an incident that illustrates the empathy between the Taos Indians and their land. A young agricultural extension agent was appointed to help them. All went well until the springtime, when the Indians suddenly became uncooperative. And this was the reason: "In the spring the Taos believe that Mother Earth is pregnant. To protect the surface of the earth they do not drive their wagons to town, they take all the shoes off their horses, they refuse to wear hardsoled shoes themselves." The extension agent, not knowing this, had tried to institute a program of early spring plowing!

With the coming of civilization this attitude was replaced by a sense of superiority of man to other living things. The book of Genesis enjoined man to have dominion over every living thing. For ages this was interpreted as a license to exploit the environment in a mood of indifference to the interests of any natural objects except man himself. "We are absolute masters," wrote Cicero, "of what the earth produces."[3] Even the animals, he said, were made for man.[4] That is how I come to call the present mood one of reconciliation. Primitive man identified himself with the environment through the beliefs of animism; modern man is once again identifying himself with the environment, this time through the evidence of science. That is my thesis. I shall now try to defend it.

My plan in these three lectures is to offer, in mere synopsis, the evidence that this trend in social values from exploitation to symbiosis is actually occurring; then to examine how these values are related to the politics of environmental protection; and finally to reflect on the evolution of the values themselves.

The Evidence for a Trend

The word "value" is the victim of arrogance from economists, obfuscation from philosophers, and rhetoric from politicians. Wilson Follett, in his book *Modern American Usage*, dismisses the word as "by now worn out and virtually without meaning." I am not competent to rescue the word from these depredations, but I shall define four different kinds of value as I use the word in these lectures.

The word "value" can mean cost in the marketplace, quantified as cash. Or it can mean usefulness, expressed as utility for persons or welfare for society. It can also mean what Locke called "intrinsick natural worth," which he sharply distinguished from cost in the marketplace; the former is an objective quality of the thing itself, the latter is its value only in relation to the value of other things that can be acquired in its stead. Finally, the word "value" can be attached, sometimes passionately, to symbols or concepts, such as a national flag or liberty. The same thing can carry all these values. Thus a piece of land has a market value; it has value-as-use for the farmer or developer; it may have intrinsic worth for its beauty; and it may be the symbol of homeland, to be defended to the death against enemies.

To illustrate that values are changing I begin with the crudest meaning of the word: the meaning attached to it by economists. The Council on Environmental Quality estimated that Federal expenditures for pollution control in the United States rose from about 0.8 billion dollars in 1969 to about 4.2 billion in 1975.[5] (And they are still rising.) Figures for other industrial nations are more modest than these, but they all show similar upward trends. In Japan the fiscal budget for environmental protection for 1974–75 was the equivalent of about 1.2 billion dollars: this was 1.8 percent of the entire government budget and an advance of 25 percent over expenditure for this purpose in 1973. In the USSR appropriations for pollution abatement doubled from 1966 to 1971.[6] This is what societies are now prepared to pay for protection of the environment.

I turn now to value as usefulness. What benefits have been purchased for these expenditures? In the United States the annual reports of the Council on Environmental Quality testify to the trends in cleaner air and water: to give one example, the dietary intake of DDT and its residues (a notorious pollutant) fell from about 70 mg per day in 1966 to about 5 mg per day in 1974.[7] In Britain the output of smoke fell from over 2 million metric tons in 1953 to half a million metric tons in 1976; the mileage of unpolluted rivers went up from 14,603 in 1958 to 17,279 in 1972, an increase of 18 percent.[8]

These two kinds of value can be quantified as dollars or milligrams or parts per million or miles of clean river. The other two kinds of value—intrinsic worth and value as symbol—play (in my view) a much more important role in man's relation to nature, but cannot be quantified without draining them of some of their content. This is an

7

assertion I shall defend later on. For the present, let me give examples to support my belief that these unqualified values, too, are changing.

The evidence comes from the study of public opinion and of social legislation, which is often the formal validation of public opinion. For generations, of course, society has been willing to protect the environment for its own ends. This is no more than self-interest. Rivers were purified in the first instance for fear of cholera and dysentery. Emissions of "noxious vapours," as they were called, were first controlled because they damaged farmland and cattle. Seasons for hunting and fishing, even support for state and national parks, are simply measures to indulge man's own activities. But self-interest is not a sufficient explanation for many recent public attitudes toward the environment. Let us spend a few minutes on one example.

In 1964, the Tees Valley and Cleveland Water Board, which was responsible for providing an adequate water supply to the great industrial area of Tees-side on the northeast coast of England, wanted to build a reservoir at a place called Cow Green in a remote and barren valley in the upper Teesdale. The reservoir was to meet the needs of expanding industry, especially to enable Imperial Chemical Industries to build the largest ammonia plant in the world.[9] There was no problem of rehousing people or dispossessing farmers; no one lived in Cow Green and the place was useless for agriculture. But the mountain turf there was the sole remaining site in England where a modest little plant called the Teesdale Sandwort, along with some other rare plants believed to be survivors from the Ice Age in Britain, could be found. The area was, therefore, of interest to botanists.

Botanists do not have the reputation of being a formidable pressure group. But some of them believed the Teesdale Sandwort and its glacial companions would be imperiled if the reservoir were built, and they rallied to protect it. A Teesdale Defence Committee was set up. Letters were written to *The Times* expressing grave anxiety about the fate of the flora. The issue was inflated into a conflict of values: on the one hand a great industry needing water (with a hint that there might be unemployment in the area if the ammonia plant could not be built there); on the other hand the "integrity" (this was one of the emotive words used) of a few acres of natural vegetation in a high and unfrequented stretch of moorland. A generation ago there would have been no doubt about the outcome of such a conflict: the Teesdale Sandwort would have stood no chance against the ammonia plant. But in the 1960's a botanical David going into battle against an industrial Goliath enlisted massive public support. The affair went to Parliament. A select committee of the House of Commons recommended that the reservoir be approved. When its report came back to the House an amendment was at once moved: "That this House declines to consider a Bill which would involve irreparable harm to a unique area of international importance." The amendment was defeated—but only by 112 votes to 82. The matter then went to the House of Lords, where it was remitted to another select committee.

This committee met 19 times and even visited the site. During the debate on the bill, which went on altogether for eight hours, there was a rational attempt to balance the cost to industry of not building the reservoir at Cow Green against the cost to science of going ahead with the reservoir. It became pretty clear that the reservoir could be built —if care were taken—without destroying the botanical interest of the area. The botanists lost; the reservoir was built; it occupies only some 6 percent of the special rock outcrop where the rare plants grow, and the Teesdale Sandwort still flourishes there. The importance of this episode was not the outcome: it was that the episode occurred at all. It was, as one politician put it, "a head-on clash between the quantifiable and the unquantifiable."

I have given you a British example because I was to some slight extent involved in it and because it would be less familiar to you than the many similar examples that abound in the United States. Of the latter, I mention only two here. One is the long-drawn-out dispute about a proposal to build a dam at Tocks Island on the Delaware River. The proposal is at present blocked, largely on the basis of unquantifiable arguments I shall discuss in a later lecture. This dispute has become a paradigm of the way value of a natural object as intrinsic worth can prevail over its economic value. The other example, familiar to Californians, is the campaign of the Sierra Club to prevent the development of a recreational center in Mineral King Valley.[10] The campaign failed in the Supreme Court, but only by a ma-

jority decision based (as I understand it) on a legal techni-
cality. Yet it led to the seminal dissenting opinion by Mr.
Justice Douglas that I mention because it is an early signal
of the way social values about the environment may become condensed into law: "Contemporary public concern
for protecting nature's ecological equilibrium should lead
to the conferral of standing upon environmental objects to
sue for their own preservation."[11] This opinion was based
on the lively essay by Christopher Stone with the provoca-
tive title *Should Trees Have Standing?*[12]

The embodiment of a social norm as law is the codifica-
tion of value-as-intrinsic-worth. The National Environmental Policy Act (NEPA) is an example, for in a pluralistic democracy such a law must reflect the social norms of
a sizable section of the population. It has imperfections, of
course, but no one can read about its operation without
seeing in it a sign of reconciliation between man and nature
in America. If you doubt this, compare it with the mood
of the American people at the time of the building of the
railroads, as described, for instance, by Leo Marx.* In Europe we have similar legislation that codifies the values
aspired to, if not yet widely held, in the European Communities. The Commission of the EEC pours out a con-

---

* Leo Marx, *The Machine in the Garden* (Oxford, 1964), p. 195,
quotes a passage from Charles Caldwell, writing in *New England Magazine* in 1832: "Alpine scenery and an embattled ocean deepen contem-
plation, and give their own sublimity to the conceptions of beholders.
The same will be true of our system of railroads. Its vastness and mag-
nificence will . . . add to the standard of the intellect of our country."

tinuous stream of draft legislation to "harmonize," in its words, the protection of the environment from the north of Scotland to the tip of Sicily. When the heads of state of the Community met in October 1972, they set the style for an environmental policy for Europe by including in their declaration the words "As befits the genius of Europe, particular attention will be given to intangible values and to protecting the environment."[13] And—a last example—the British Parliament recently passed an act making it an offense to kill, injure, or have in one's possession any of 21 plants (including the Teesdale Sandwort) and six creatures (including the natterjack toad), although it is unlikely that any of those who debated and voted for the bill had seen any of the animals or plants it protects.[14]

To clinch my argument I should take you back into the nineteenth and early twentieth centuries to demonstrate that the public attitude to nature and to the environment, as measured in all four meanings of the word "value" I have used, has evolved over the last two or three generations from indifference toward concern. I have elsewhere analyzed this trend in the social attitudes toward smoke abatement in Britain.[15] For the present I ask you to accept that we *are* witnessing a trend. Of course the reconciliation of man with nature is not accomplished. There is still reckless exploitation of some nonrenewable resources. There is still obstinate opposition from some vested interests. It needed only a threat to our comfort, such as was given by OPEC in 1973, to erode our altruism toward the environment in Alaska. But there is indubitable evidence of an adaptation of social values to anticipate some of the dangers of environmental decay. Those who preach environmental doom do a disservice to their cause when they neglect this evidence, for by studying exactly how this adaptation is taking place we may find means to accelerate it and to extend it to other social hazards.

If I have one paramount misgiving about books on the so-called ecological crisis, it involves their use of the word "must." "Economic and technologic considerations," writes René Dubos, "must be made subservient to the needs, attributes, and aspirations that have been woven into the fabric of man's nature."[16] "We must," writes E. F. Schumacher, "learn to think in terms of an articulated structure that can cope with a multiplicity of small-scale units."[17] "Long-term goals," write Meadows and his co-workers, "must be specified and short-term goals made consistent with them."[18] And "modern man," write Paul and Anne Ehrlich, "must come soon to a better understanding of the Earth and of what he has been doing to it."[19] The sentiments are not misguided; it is just that they are empty rhetoric unless they are accompanied by specific and politically feasible—and I repeat *specific and politically feasible*—plans for turning "must be" into "can be." That politics is the art of the possible is a cliché, but those who have not mastered that art cannot expect their political prescriptions to be taken seriously. I invite you therefore to approach these issues from another direction. Let us not talk about what *must* happen; let us examine exactly what *does* happen when a decision is made to protect the environment.

The Chain Reaction

Between the disclosure of an environmental hazard and political action to control the hazard there is a complex chain reaction of events. The public conscience is excited; public-interest lobbies mobilize to defend the environment; self-interest lobbies set out to stop decisions that threaten their interests. Among those who have responsibility for dealing with the hazard there is an inbuilt inertia manifested as stalling questions: "Is this just a passing scare?" "Will the problem go away if we take no notice of it?" When it becomes clear that the problem will not go away, the responsible body (politician or administrative agency) seeks advice from experts in science and from experts in economics. In due course the experts give their opinions, the lobbies deliver their volleys of advocacy, and the politician has to make a decision that may ultimately be codified in law.

This chain reaction is complex, but it can be simplified into three stages. In the first stage—let us call it the ignition stage—public opinion has to be raised to a temperature that stimulates political action. In the second stage the hazard has to be examined objectively, to find out how genuine and how dangerous it is, and just what is at risk. In the third stage this objective information has to be combined with the pressures of advocacy and with subjective judgments to produce a formula for a political decision. We can, therefore, think of the chain reaction as an initial ignition of the issue followed by inputs. The inputs of the scientist and the economist are assumed to be objective (some say "value-free," but we shall come to that later), whereas the inputs of spokesmen for public and private interests are known to be subjective; to these is added the politician's input, which includes not only facts but "hunch." In the two lectures after this one I shall reflect on the value problems that confront the scientist, the economist, and the politician. For the rest of this lecture let us look at the ignition stage—the excitation of the public conscience.

Excitation of the Public Conscience

Here the value problems are different from those in the succeeding stages. They are a consequence of living in a pluralistic democracy. In a dictatorship the responsible authority is not obliged to secure consensus from the public before banning a pesticide or building a dam. In a democracy, though, it is a case of "no consensus, no votes." It is not enough simply to disclose an environmental hazard; public opinion has to be mobilized to press for action to deal with it. Translated into the terms of these lectures, this means that social values—in all four senses of the word "value"—have to be lifted to such a level that the people on whose support politicians rely will not tolerate the abuse of the environment and will show themselves willing to make some sacrifice to protect it.

Environmental hazards are disclosed either by some incident that shocks the public or by some discovery made by scientists. In the first category were the 1948 smog in Donora, Pennsylvania, and the 1952 London smog that caused some 4,000 deaths. Another case in Britain was the disclosure that drums that had contained cyanide were being dumped in places where they could poison water supplies or children; and another recent case in America was the outbreak of illness among cattle following the accidental proliferation of a fire retardant, PBB (polybrominated biphenyl), in the state of Michigan.[20] In the second category are hazards that might have passed unnoticed but for the prescience of scientists. An early example of this was the prediction made by the American geologist T. C. Chamberlain in 1899 that the burning of fossil fuels would increase the concentration of carbon dioxide in the atmosphere, which might in turn cause a rise in the temperature of the earth's surface. Recent examples are the discovery that polychlorinated biphenyls (PCBs), which have been used since 1929 in industry, were escaping into the environment and accumulating in the food chain and causing injury to animals and to man;[21] and the prediction made by Molina and Rowland in 1974 that fluorocarbons in aerosol sprays might destroy the ozone in the stratosphere that protects us from an excess of ultraviolet radiation.[22] Unless the media give saturation treatment to the story, the chief agent for alerting the public is the public-interest lobby. These lobbies play an essential part in the chain reaction. Their influence depends upon the reputation they gain for integrity. Thus in America the Sierra Club and in Britain the Conservation Society and the National Society for Clean Air have a high reputation and are correspondingly effective.

The process of the ignition of public opinion poses ethical problems. Let me illustrate this by two examples. In 1970 a report sponsored by the Massachusetts Institute of Technology was published under the title *Man's Impact on the Global Environment: Report of the Study of Critical Environmental Problems.*[23] It was a sober, well-documented, clearly written study, and it became known as the SCEP Report. It is still the best summary of these problems. It made some recommendations that, as one reviewer put it, were "neither utopian nor apocalyptic." One aspect of the report, wrote another reviewer, was "its humility. It does not attempt to ring the doomsday bell."

The report received respectful attention from environmental scientists but caused no ripple of response from the public. Some months later, in January 1972, a journal called *The Ecologist* published an issue entitled *A Blueprint for Survival.*[24] The data in the *Blueprint* were taken largely from the SCEP Report, but unlike that report the *Blueprint* was both utopian and apocalyptic, and it rang the doomsday bell with frantic vigor. It used sensational and emotive prose to get its message across. On practically every page there were assertions repugnant to the rational reader: plunges into naive fallacies; innuendoes; patently incorrect assertions; and statements unsupported by published and accepted evidence. The *Blueprint* was lavish with prescriptions of what "must" be done, with scarcely any reference to what "was" being done and, more important, to *how* it was being done. Reports of the Royal Commission on Environmental Pollution and the Council on Environmental Quality, for instance, were not even included in the list of references.

Now I come to the point. *A Blueprint for Survival* is a travesty of the authoritative and impressive SCEP Report. But, unlike that report, it made a great impact on the British public. Television programs were built around it. Editorials were written about it. The Secretary of State for the Environment, with appropriate publicity, went to the trouble of inviting some of the signatories to the *Blueprint* to meet him. It excited the public conscience.

Now for the second example. In the summer of 1963, on a couple of farms in southeast England, some sheep and cattle and a foxhound died. The postmortem showed that they had been poisoned by fluorocetamide, which was traced to a field next to a factory that produced pesticides. The factory dumped drums and canisters and allowed them to rust away in this field, which drained into some ponds on the farms where the animals were likely to drink.

The incident caused no great stir, but it did lead the Minister of Housing and Local Government to appoint a Technical Committee on the Disposal of Toxic Solid Wastes to advise what changes were desirable in order to ensure safe disposal without risk of polluting water supplies and rivers. The committee set to work in a leisurely manner: it met 20 times over a stretch of six years and produced in the spring of 1970 a lifeless and tedious report that did, however, conclude that existing legislation on toxic wastes was inadequate.[25] The report got scant notice in the media, and nothing was done.

Meanwhile Britain, along with other industrial countries, was becoming environment-conscious. In 1970 a Royal Commission on Environmental Pollution was appointed, with wide powers of enquiry. Its first task was to survey the state of the environment in Britain. It found evidence of "fly-tipping," that is, the illicit dumping of toxic wastes in places not registered to receive them; and it urged the government to tighten the law.[26] Still nothing was done. Throughout 1971 the Royal Commission collected further examples of fly-tipping, and in August it expressed disquiet at the potential danger to water supplies and the government's failure to deal with the matter. The government's reply was that there was too heavy a program of parliamentary business for the matter to be dealt with in the coming session; moreover, there was to be a reorganization of local government that would affect the administrative arrangements, and a comprehensive bill to control pollution was to be introduced sometime in 1974. In October and November 1971, further pressure was brought on the Minister by the Royal Commission, and on November 30, the chairman of the Royal Commission wrote to the Minister to say that "the risk to the public is such that we must pursue this matter, even though it is at an awkward time." Still no action was taken, and the Commission drafted a report critical of the government that was published on March 7, 1972.[27] But before that date a new character had appeared in the story. His name was Lonnie Downes. He was a truck driver in a waste-disposal firm in the Midlands and shop steward for his branch of the Transport and General Workers Union. He discovered that some of his mates were being given a bonus of £20 a week for dumping loads of cyanide, chromic acid, caustic soda, phenol, and other noxious substances on delivery tickets that described them as harmless "suds oil." Mr. Downes complained to the management of the firm, who replied with vague threats of dismissal. A few weeks later Mr. Downes was offered promotion, which he declined. Then, so it was reported, he was offered £300 if he would leave the company; again he declined. Instead, he reported the whole affair to the local branch of the Conservation Society. The Society, helped by specific information from Mr. Downes and his mates, prepared a detailed report and sent it to the Secretary of State for the Environment.[28] Still nothing was done.

At this point the Conservation Society, having given due warning that it would make the matter public, sent its findings to the press. The story broke in the Birmingham *Sunday Mercury* on January 10, 1972. Thereafter press, radio, and television descended upon the refuse dumps of Britain like a flock of scavenging birds. Pictures of alleged toxic waste drums appeared in the newspapers. Parliament was forced to hold a special debate on the issue, but the Under Secretary of State still maintained that the parliamentary timetable was too packed for legislation to be introduced before 1974.

Toward the end of February 1972 the government knew

that the Royal Commission was about to publish its views on toxic wastes; but on February 24 an incident occurred that eclipsed the sober deliberations of a Royal Commission. Thirty-six one-hundredweight drums were discovered in a derelict piece of ground near the town of Nuneaton, on a site where children played. Attempts had been made to erase the label 'sodium cyanide' from the drums and some of the crystals were sticking to the outside. The Department of the Environment hurriedly drafted a bill to control the deposit of poisonous waste. It was read for the first time on March 8, went through its remaining stages on March 16, and passed into law on March 30.

I tell this story to illustrate the vagaries of the human dimension in the first stage of the chain reaction between the disclosure of an environmental hazard and political action to control it. The moral of the story was aptly summed up in an editorial in *The Times* when the emergency bill was introduced:

It is instructive to note what did and what did not prompt the Government to squeeze a Bill as a matter of urgency into an already crowded legislative programme. The urgent representations of an official commission composed of distinguished persons who were moved by "the disturbing cases which have come to our knowledge of local problems and anxieties" did not. Headlines about drums of cyanide waste on derelict land in the Midlands did.[29]

It is one consequence of the astonishing adaptability of man that he has to be persuaded to be dissatisfied about abuses to his environment. To set the chain reaction going is often the hardest task in social reform. This raises an ethical problem of some importance. Is it morally defensible to use shock tactics, to exaggerate, to distort the facts or color them with emotive words, or to slant the television camera in order to excite the public conscience? My experience leads me reluctantly to believe that *in the present social climate* some dramatization is necessary. Without Rachel Carson public apathy about the hazards of pesticides might have persisted for a decade longer. Without the computerized jeremiads published by Meadows and his associates the public might not yet have been alerted to the ominous consequences of unregulated consumption in affluent countries. But notice an important point about these enthusiasts: they are commonly what academics call "unsound," which in academia is a highly pejorative epithet. Rachel Carson's biology can be faulted, and she uses cunningly the technique of a storyteller in her opening chapter. Meadows's computer simulations deserve the description attached to them by one reviewer: "The computer that printed out W.O.L.F." And yet, if these writers had been coolly rational, if they had stuck meticulously to uncolored verifiable facts, would they have made any impression on the public conscience? I doubt it, and my doubts are confirmed by the opinions of two very great men, one a philosopher and the other a theologian. It was Alfred North Whitehead who made the surprising assertion that "It is more important that a proposition be interesting than that it be true."[30] Propositions hedged about with reservations, as many scientific statements have to be, are seldom interesting to the public. And Cardinal Newman was even more emphatic: "Deductions," he wrote, "have no power of persuasion. . . . Many a man will live and die upon a dogma; no man will be a martyr for a conclusion."*

I said that I believed this compromise with objectivity to be necessary "in the present social climate." Compromise has not always been necessary. Before the days of universal suffrage the range of public opinion that had to be satisfied was much narrower. The small minority of people who read national newspapers were willing (to judge from the format of those papers) to plow through enormous, closely argued paragraphs that appealed to the head rather than to the heart. If a rational case could be made that some abuse of the environment was a hazard to health or property, and if control of the abuse did not threaten the interests of powerful people, then governments were willing to pass laws to protect the environment—though of course out of self-interest, not for altruistic motives. Let me give you an example to illustrate this.

It concerns the campaign conducted by a pioneer for public health in Britain, John Simon, over a century ago. In 1848 he was appointed the first medical officer of health

* J. H. Newman, *Discussions and Arguments on Various Subjects* (London, 1872), p. 295. The context of this surprising remark was an innocent speech by Sir Robert Peel in opening a library at Tamworth. Peel extolled the moral virtues of learning (as a politician might be expected to do when opening a library) and gave the impression that secular knowledge could be as effective a principle for moral improvement as religious knowledge could, and that "an increased sagacity" in science could support religious faith. This Newman denied, in a letter to *The Times*.

for the City of London. The sanitary state of London was appalling. Here is a description of a sight in the East End written by Mayhew for the *Morning Chronicle* in September 1849:

We passed along the reeking banks of the sewer. . . . We were assured this was the only water the wretched inhabitants had to drink, [and] we saw drains and sewers emptying their filthy contents into it. . . . A whole tier of doorless privies [was] built over it, [and] the limbs of the vagrant boys bathing in it seemed by pure force of contrast white as Parian marble. . . . We were taken to a house where an infant lay dead of the cholera. We asked if they *really did* drink the water. The answer was, "They were obliged to drink the ditch, without they could beg a pailful or thieve a pailful of water."

Simon realized as clearly as anyone that his problem was to raise the social value attached to cleanliness among the common people. "For rich and poor alike," he wrote, "there must be sufficient refinement of taste to abhor even minor degrees of dirt, and to insist throughout on the utmost possible purity of air and water." But his strategy for exciting the public conscience was never to exaggerate, never to make assertions that could not be supported by hard facts; and in the social climate of those times this was sufficient. Here is the comment of *The Times* on Simon's first annual report to the City, published on November 8, 1849, two months after Mayhew's description I have just quoted:

Mr. Simon's report to the City Commissioners of Sewers is unquestionably the ablest, most lucid, and most temperate statement of our sanitary condition and wants that it has yet been our fortune to peruse; and we are greatly mistaken if it is not the programme of an earnest movement and the foundation of a substantial reform. What we wish to call the attention of our readers to in this report, and what constitutes its real power, is the care taken by Mr. Simon to state all his facts in the most simple and undeniable form. By avoiding all exaggeration, by contenting himself with the lowest estimate of facts and their consequences, he presents no assailable points to those critics who take up the subject for no other purpose than to create a diversion.

Simon's campaign was not, of course, to reconcile man with nature; it was to improve health. But it was an early lesson to British society that if the environment is abused, health and property may suffer. The motive for action was not symbiosis with nature but fear of retaliation from nature. Simon succeeded because he convinced people that cholera and dysentery were linked to contaminated water. His measures to clean up the air had to overcome two difficulties. For one thing, the link between smoke and disease was less evident; for another, to get furnaces to "consume their own smoke" would have meant costs to commerce. So there was a conflict of values: on the one hand was market value, epitomized in the Victorian phrase "Where there's muck there's brass"; on the other hand was value as intrinsic worth and symbol, the embarrassment that an "ignoble pall of unconsumed soot" (as Simon called it) shrouded the capital of a proud empire.

Proposals to protect the environment almost always provoke such conflicts. On one side are those who stand to lose if the responsible authority imposes any kind of constraint upon their activities for the sake of the environment; on the other side are self-appointed custodians of what they regard as the common good, who urge the authority to act. To be effective each side has to organize itself into a lobby—the one to protect self-interest, the other to protect the public interest. Each side engages in frankly tendentious advocacy to advance its cause. This adversary process, eagerly publicized by the media, helps to ignite public opinion.

The politician is the target of this advocacy, for he has to decide what is the common good and to hold a balance between private and public interests. He obviously cannot rely on the *ex parte* pleading of the lobbies as his sole evidence for making a political decision. Before the chain reaction can proceed further, there has to be an objective, unbiased input of hard data to combine with the subjective input of opinions and prejudices in order to dissolve any distortions of fact that may have been used by the media or the lobbies to ignite public opinion and to disclose whether there is any residue that justifies political action. For this unbiased input the politician turns to the scientist and the economist. Their part in the chain reaction is the topic of my next lecture.

TWO

Objective Components of the Chain Reaction

In the first lecture I gave a simple model of the chain reaction from disclosure of a hazard to the environment to action to cope with the hazard, which will be my subject in the third lecture. In the space of an hour I tried to give sufficient evidence to persuade you that there is a trend in social values—distinguishable from capricious fluctuations in taste—toward greater concern for the environment, whether the values have to do with the marketplace, or utility, or intrinsic worth shading into a symbolic value attached to the conservation of natural objects. The trend is toward a mood that opposes not only sources of pollution such as power stations and paper mills, but also defacements of the landscape, such as reservoirs and highways. These social values, combined with facts, influence political action.

I then invited you to consider some of the facts and values that enter into each stage of the chain reaction. We began with the initial stage, which I called the ignition of public concern. At this stage the bare facts are interlaced with emotive epithets; cautious speculations by scientists are distorted to appear as established facts; the consequences of some potential hazard are dramatized. The motives of the mass media in doing this are to make news. Since the public will not respond to anything that is not news, the would-be protector of the environment is faced with an ethical problem: Is it legitimate to dramatize some potential environmental hazard in order to overcome indifference among the public? I suggested—though reluctantly—that in the present social climate, when these techniques of the mass media are used to alert the public to all sorts of issues from corruption in politics to abuses in medical care, there is no alternative but to concede their use over environmental issues. Without persuasion the public would be informed but not alerted. In the days when political decisions could be made without much regard to public opinion, this did not matter. Today, when the public—informed by the mass media—demand to be consulted before political decisions are made, it does matter that they should be alerted. Hence the sensational phrases (e.g., "Lake Erie is dead"); the television cameras focused on dead fish or littered beer cans; the innuendos about DDT poisoning children. These set the chain reaction going. Let us now consider the next stage of the reaction.

Responsibility for doing something about an environmental hazard rests with some authority: central or local government, or an agency such as the Environmental Protection Agency in America or a regional water authority in England. Under pressure from public-interest lobbies and from politicians anxious for the common good, the authority has to act. There is a useful distinction (drawn by Passmore) between *ecological problems,* which are primarily social and political, and *problems in ecology,* which are narrowly scientific.[1] It is for scientists to say whether there is a hazard to the environment and what its cause is; it is for administrators and politicians to decide what to do in the public interest about the alleged hazard. The scientific question—the problem in ecology—has to be answered first. Hard facts have to be dissected out of the distorted reporting of the hazard. So a common practice is for the responsible politician to appoint a committee of scientists and technologists to assess the problem and to make a report.

The Scientist's Input

Let me illustrate this by an example. There is at present worldwide concern about the accumulation of fluorocarbons in the atmosphere. These are chemicals used as propellants in hairsprays, deodorants, perfumes, insecticides, paints, and polishers; they are used also in refrigerators, air conditioners, and plastic foams. About three-quarters of the fluorocarbons released into the atmosphere come from spray-propellants. World production of the two commonest kinds (known as CFC 12 and CFC 11) rose from about 50,000 metric tons per year in 1950 to about 800,000 metric tons in 1974.[2]

In 1974 two American scientists suggested that these chemicals probably ascend to the stratosphere (30–50 kilometers above the earth) and decompose there in a way that may slowly destroy some of the ozone layer protecting the earth from an excess of ultraviolet radiation.[3] If this protection were weakened, the excess of radiation might affect human health (it is known to be a cause of skin cancer), and vegetation and climate. Here is a case where the hazard was not disclosed by some calamity; it was disclosed, long before it had become a hazard, by the foresight of scientists.

Of course once the media took it up, the hazard was dramatized. Headlines such as "Peril from Aerosols," "Cancer Threat," and "Crisis in the Stratosphere" alerted the public and set the chain reaction briskly in motion. The self-interest lobby took defensive action (e.g., there was a two-page advertisement in *Harper's Magazine* for November 1975, assuring the public that the risk was being exaggerated and that the problem was being studied in a dozen different universities). The public-interest lobby started campaigns to ban aerosols. In 1975 the Council on Environmental Policy published a report by the Federal Task Force on Inadvertent Modification of the Stratosphere (IMOS, a body that had been active over the possible effects of supersonic aircraft),[4] and in 1976 a committee of the National Research Council presented to the National Academy of Sciences a comprehensive scientific assessment of the problem.[5] At the same time in Britain the Secretary of State for the Environment sought advice from experts on atmospheric chemistry, whose findings were published in 1976.[6]

I shall not burden you with the scientific complexity of the problem, for that is not the purpose of these lectures. I shall use the example to reflect on the assumptions about values that are made when scientific advice is given to governments. Any decision to phase out the release of fluorocarbons would have had far-reaching economic and political consequences, so it is essential at this stage of the chain reaction to disentangle fact-statements from value-statements. Scientific advice is assumed to be rigorously confined to fact-statements; the authority of the expert is technical, not moral. The scientist does not deal with reality; he deals with arbitrary abstractions from reality that he expresses as symbols. For example, the phosphate content of a lake is symbolized as milligrams per liter; the lead-level in blood as micrograms per 100 milliliters; the level of ultraviolet radiation as photons per square centimeter per second. These are the scientist's input into the chain reaction. They are symbols, and they are assumed to be value-free. But it is not so simple to separate fact-statements from value-statements. Let us consider three difficulties.

First, the scientist does not deal with the whole crystal of reality; he deals only with one facet at a time. Problems in ecology are complex; the only way to tackle them is to simplify them; and the only way to simplify them is to leave out what you consider to be the less relevant information. So when a scientist gives you an opinion it is important to ask him what simplifications he has made. Here is an example. In order to issue regulations to control discharges into rivers, authorities responsible for fisheries ask scientists how much oxygen there has to be in a river for fish to flourish. There is no simple answer to this question. It depends on the species of fish. It depends on the stage of growth of the fish: 5 mg of oxygen per liter may be enough for eggs to hatch; but for good growth in the earliest stages fish may need 7 mg per liter; yet later on, 3 mg per liter may be enough. Shad will migrate upstream at 2 mg per liter but will not form a school at oxygen levels below 5 mg per liter. The oxygen level will be affected, too, by temperature, vegetation in the water, the depth of the river, even the speed of wind blowing across the surface. All this is too complicated for the politician. What he wants is a single figure. He gets one (e.g., the European Community quality standard for water supporting coarse fish is 5 mg of oxygen per liter). But—and this is the point that has to be remembered—this is a value-statement as well as a fact-statement, for it includes the scientist's judgment of what he could safely leave out when he simplified the problem.

Second, the responsible authority may not appreciate the reservations in the scientist's advice. The politician, beset by pressure groups and inclined to act like a seismograph recording public opinion, wants from the scientist an unambiguous answer to his question. What foreign substance is threatening the environment? How much of it is there? How much damage will that amount cause? How much damage will be done if no action is taken? The scientist's answer comes in symbols that to the layman have a welcome air of precision. This is deceptive.

True, some phenomena in science can be predicted with near certainty, e.g., that in the latitude of London the sun will rise on Saturday, October 15, 1977, at 7:23 A.M. But this degree of precision is very rare in the environmental sciences. Almost all fact-statements in this kind of science are not facts at all: they are gambles on the likelihood of something happening. So attached to the input of symbols from the scientists are words such as "might" and "possibly," with (so to speak) betting odds attached; and the difficulty, which I shall discuss more fully in my next lecture, is that the politician and the public attempt to attribute more precision to scientific advice than the advice carries if you read the reservations. This is what is happening over the question whether or not to ban fluorocarbons in aerosols. A decision to delay any regulation for two years, from 1977 to 1979, would alter the ozone depletion at any later date by no more than one-sixth of one percent.[7] But day by day the concentration of ozone in the stratosphere varies, from natural causes, by up to 25 percent; moreover, there are variations in the ozone concentration with distance from the poles, with season of the year, and with a kind of rhythm over 20–40 months. Discovering a trend of depletion of ozone owing to aerosol residues within these large fluctuations is indeed looking for a needle in a cosmic haystack. It was estimated (when scientists were trying to find how to measure the effects of supersonic flights on the ozone layer) that it would take six years of observations to be able to say, with 95 percent confidence, that the ozone layer was being depleted at the rate of 5 percent per year.[8] I mention this to illustrate with what fastidious caution, with what underlining of reservations, the scientist surrounds his input into the decision-making process. The temptation of the journalist who writes the story for the public, and for the politician who has to interpret public opinion, is to strip off all the conditions surrounding the evidence, and to say simply that aerosols destroy the ozone layer, which in turn will (not "may") increase skin cancer, which is sufficient to demand an immediate ban on the use of fluorocarbons. The scientific evidence certainly justifies the working out of plans to phase out the use of these chemicals in aerosols over the next few years; it does not justify panic legislation that would suddenly disrupt a large industry. This is another difficulty about the assumption that the scientific evidence is value-free. An indisputable fact (e.g., that this sample of air contains so much ozone) *is* value-free;* but as soon as you say there is a 20-percent chance of so much ozone being present you are expressing numerically a degree of belief, you are making a value judgment. When you make predictions from probabilities (and this is what advice entails) you are assuming that the thing you have measured will continue to behave as consistently in the future as it did in the past. This assumption is well founded for simple physical situations; it is unlikely to be well founded for complex ecological situations. So even though a fact-statement expressed in the symbolism of science may be regarded as value-free, the process of interpreting the implications of the statement is not. It contains subtle assumptions about the statistical chances of a cause producing an effect. Without these assumptions the fact-statement is not valid; yet it is this cause-effect relationship that the politician needs to know in order to make a decision. So in

---

* Apart, of course, from its value-as-usefulness, and from the value judgment implicit in all science and scholarship that truth, however unpalatable it may be, is preferable to error, however convenient it may be.

giving advice the scientist has to reinstate all the reservations and qualifications that may have been stripped off by the mass media (and sometimes the lobbies) in their efforts to make news value out of the environmental issue. It is not surprising that one American senator is reported to have said "I wish I could have advice from a one-armed scientist, who won't tell me something and then say 'on the other hand.' "

The third difficulty in separating fact-statements from value-statements is that the scientist may not have been asked the right question (by "right" I mean the question that will provide the answer needed for a political decision). Thus, to use an example familiar to Americans, in the 1960's scientists were asked the question, Does phosphate endanger the biological balance of lakes, and if so what can be put into detergents in place of phosphate that will not harm lakes? Their reply was yes, excess of phosphate does harm some lakes, and yes, a substance called NTA (sodium nitrilo-triacetate) could replace phosphate in detergents and would not harm lakes. On the strength of this reply several American states took political action to phase out phosphate from detergents. It was only later that the scientists added to their reply a piece of information for which they had not been asked, namely that under some circumstances NTA in drinking water *might* cause cancer; at that point the Surgeon General of the United States banned NTA from detergents, and the states' political action had to be put into reverse.

So the scientist often has to reinterpret the question on

which he has been asked to give advice in the light of the social or political purpose behind it. This is his clear moral responsibility; but there is no doubt that it may draw him into the arena of value-conflicts, beyond the authority he carries because he is an expert. To balance the undoubted benefit of cutting down the flow of phosphates into lakes against the possible risk of NTA to human health is an equation that cannot be solved by science; it is a political equation. Yet the objective inputs into the equation come from scientists. What influence do they have on the way their inputs are used? This is a question that has long troubled the conscience of scientists. Shelfloads of books have been written about what they ought to do. My present concern is not with "ought" but with what actually happens at this point in the chain reaction from environmental hazard to political action.

There is no formal code of practice for the scientific adviser, but anyone in the business who reflects on the assumptions he makes can distinguish some legitimate value-judgments implicit in his contribution. First, of the four kinds of values I distinguished in the first lecture, the input expected from the scientist is *value-as-usefulness*. Thus it is useful for the decision-maker to know that the amount of lead in the ice cap in Greenland has increased twenty-fold in the last 200 years. The scientist therefore bears in mind that his advice is in this category of value; the reliability and credibility of his advice rests on his capacity as a reductionist, whatever his private philosophy may be. He is expected therefore to avoid comment on value-as-market-cost, which is the economist's business, just as he is expected to avoid comment on value-as-intrinsic-worth, which it is the business of the public-interest lobbies to offer. On the whole, the more he sticks to this principle, the more weight his opinion carries.

Second, within the category of value-as-usefulness there are subsets of value judgments; these, too, are legitimately included in the scientist's advice. Thus he expresses a judgment about the confidence that can be placed in the data. (How reliable was the technique? How representative were the samples taken?) He expresses, too, a judgment about the relevance of the data for the given purpose of the political decision, and he may go beyond his brief to indicate "overtone" scientific consequences that may follow a decision made on the data he provides (e.g., that aerosols, quite apart from possible damage to the ozone layer, might seriously affect the climate).

Finally, there are issues on which the scientist is uniquely qualified to act as moral witness, questioning the ends for which he has been asked to offer the means. Normally the political authority defines ends (e.g., the extent to which nature shall be exploited for the benefit of man) and the scientist is consulted over means. Since Francis Bacon proclaimed *tantum possumus, quantum scimus*—"we can do as much as we know"—the paradigm in industrial societies has been "what we know how to do, we shall do." We have applied it to nuclear energy and supersonic flight, and we stand on the brink of applying it to genetic engineering. But here, again owing to the prescience of some scientists, we hesitate, and this is a sign that the paradigm is changing, as it changed when scientists turned from the study of final causes to the study of proximal causes four centuries ago. We are now, on the initiative of scientists themselves, questioning whether we ought to do as much as we know how to do, not only for our own safety but for the security of nature as a whole—other living things, mineral resources, the landscape. This emerging attitude is a sign of a reconciliation of man with nature; it is about value as intrinsic worth; it is already having some effect on the ways science is applied to social ends, and it might even influence the policies for scientific research. It is important, however, to keep this activity of scientists as critics of value-as-intrinsic-worth separate from their day-to-day activity in the environmental chain reaction as advisers on value-as-usefulness.

The Economist's Input

In the second report of the Council on Environmental Quality there is a striking diagram.[9] It shows the marginal cost of purifying the effluent from a sugar beet factory.* To remove up to 30 percent of the polluting matter costs marginally less than $1 per pound of pollutant removed. To remove 65 percent of the polluting matter would cost marginally something like $20 per pound of pollutant removed. Hence to double the level of purification would raise the cost 20 times. Another example comes from a United Na-

---

* I.e., the cost at any level of purification (say 50 percent) of increasing the amount of purification by another step (say by 5 percent more).

tions symposium.[10] The Delaware estuary is so badly polluted that in the summer months there is not enough oxygen in the water to sustain a good population of fish. It is estimated that it would cost about $1.6 million a year with a capital outlay of some $120 million to raise the oxygen level to 2 parts per million. But to double this—to raise the oxygen level to 4 parts per million—would cost annually nearly 4.5 times as much and would require a $300 million capital outlay.

These examples are typical. The cost of protecting the environment rises very steeply with the level of protection. There must come a limit of cost above which even the most dedicated conservationist would consider further expenditure unreasonable. What is a reasonable cost? To get an answer to this question the politician turns to the economist.

Permit me a brief digression about economists. Like scientists, they convey their information in symbols, not as milligrams or probabilities but as money. They use money because it is a convenient symbol to measure the preferences of people when they have to make choices. Unfortunately, money has all sorts of overtones. It is not only a convenient symbol used by economists to express value in the marketplace; it is also the symbol of an ideology, denoting the values of a materialist culture. This confusion in the use of money as a symbol makes economists vulnerable to misunderstanding. In a moment I shall be critical of some economists, so I want now to say a word in their defense.

Economists, as one of them wrote, deal with "logical

deductions from a set of definitions and assumptions. . . that may or may not be ethical in nature."[11] They are concerned with the logic of choice. Individuals and societies are confronted every day with the need to make choices. Some are trivial choices, involving, for example, whether to have chicken or beef for a $6 dinner; some are serious choices, involving whether or not to build a pipeline across Alaska. The economist's axioms are, first, that choice is commonly unavoidable (if you have only $6 to spend on a meal, you cannot have both chicken and beef); second, that choice is rational (even if you use an apparently irrational mode of choice, such as tossing a coin to decide between chicken and beef, it means your preferences for the two are exactly equal, which is indeed rational); and third, that preferences even for things not for sale in the market can nevertheless still be expressed by the common surrogate for barter, namely money. The economist sets out the logical consequences of allocating resources this way or that way; he does not moralize over which way the resources ought to be allocated. Pollution is no more "good" or "bad" to him than cyanide is "good" or "bad" to a chemist. But just as the chemist can tell you, in a weight-symbol, how much cyanide has been dumped in a pit, so the economist can tell you, in a money-symbol, what it will cost to dispose of the cyanide in some other way.[12]

The economist's most important contribution to environmental policy is contained in the clumsy phrase "internalizing the externalities." When people owned slaves, labor was free apart from the capital cost of buying the slaves and the running cost of feeding and clothing them. When the public conscience would no longer tolerate slavery, the cost of labor began to be internalized—the wage bill was added to the cost of the product. This did not complete the process of internalization, for labor was still exploited until it became a scarce resource.

Exploitation of the environment is following a similar process. Until recently wastes could be discharged free into air and water, which nobody owned; and land, once it had been acquired, could be exploited without restraint. The public conscience will no longer tolerate this; the government is expected to protect air, water, and land against irresponsible exploitation. The costs of disposing of wastes have begun to be internalized, and the bill for pollution abatement is being added to the cost of the product. This process of internalization is by no means complete. It is only in the last decade or so that an undamaged environment has become, as it were, a scarce resource, and that the public-interest movement to protect the environment— the analogue of trade unions for labor—has become powerful enough to put constraints on the exploitation of the environment.

No one would now deny that the real cost of any enterprise, from the generation of energy to the manufacture of detergents, must include its indirect costs to society, which include the cost of protecting the environment from damage or defacement. The principle that externalities should be internalized is accepted, but the translation of it into practice presents all sorts of difficulties. A major difficulty is

43

relevant to these lectures: it is a problem in value-judgment.

This problem arises from the question I asked just now: What is a reasonable price to pay for protecting the environment? The economist has an elegant theoretical answer to this question. The marginal cost of protecting the environment increases steeply as the level of protection is raised. By similar logic it can be said that the marginal damage done if the environment is not protected will decrease as the level of protection is raised. If the marginal cost of damage is plotted on the same graph as the marginal cost of protection, the two curves will cross (see Figure 1). The point where they cross is the *optimum* expenditure to protect the environment: any expenditure above this point costs more than the cost of the damage it saves; and below this point the cost of the damage will always exceed the cost of paying to prevent it. Thus, in the figure, the optimum amount of pollutant to be removed is shown as *P* percent at a marginal cost *C*.

I called this an elegant theoretical answer. But it contains a flaw, for these two curves are about different kinds of value. The cost-of-treatment curve (*T*) is straightforward: it measures what has to be paid in the market to install and run a sewage plant, or to extract sulphur from oil, or to cut down on the emission of noxious gases from the exhausts of automobiles, or to put power cables underground instead of defacing the skyline with them. This curve is about value as economists use the word. But the cost-of-damage curve (*D*) is not straightforward, for it is compounded of three kinds of value: money, usefulness, and intrinsic

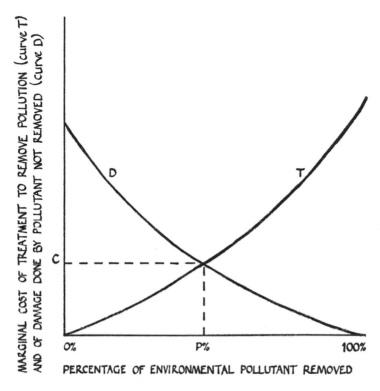

FIGURE I. Percentage of Environmental Pollutant Removed. Marginal cost of treatment to remove pollution (curve T) and of damage done by pollutant not removed (curve D).

worth. Some of the damage can be assessed in money terms without transformation: e.g., if people downstream want to drink the river water, their purification system will cost more if the river is polluted upstream. If the river is too polluted to carry fish it can be argued—though it is stretch-

45

ing a point—that the transport costs of local fishermen to other fishing grounds is an element of the damage cost in the polluted river. But what is the market value of the river's lost beauty, the damage to waterfowl and plants, and the legacy of squalor that present neglect may bequeath to future generations? In short, what about the value of the river as intrinsic worth?

Before I try to answer these questions, consider another example: the damage caused by air pollution. Plausible estimates can be made of the additional costs for laundry, painting, and replacement of corroded metal and stone in a smoke-laden as opposed to a clean city. It is possible, too, though with arguable assumptions, to estimate the harm to human health of life under a pall of smoke: the costs of medical care for respiratory diseases, days lost from work, even premature death. But what is the dollar cost of drabness, of the tensions and distress in the home of a chronic invalid with emphysema? In short, what about the value of clean air as intrinsic worth?

These questions are not rhetorical. Reference to them must be included in the advice the economist gives to the politician because that advice, based on a balancing of costs against benefits, may be used to frame a law, or to fix subsidies to industry, or to set levels for taxing pollution. The economist has two options. On the one hand, he can accompany his advice with a warning that his cost-benefit analysis includes only easily quantifiable terms and omits fragile values whose quantification would be little more than guesswork. The politician then knows the boundaries of the advice he is getting and knows that it is up to him to supply the missing parts from some other source. On the other hand, the economist can translate the fragile values into presumptive money values and assure the politician that he has included all relevant data in his analysis. This is a common practice. Let us see how it is done.

Five years ago a thorough study was made of the social cost of air pollution in Britain.[13] The country was divided into clean and dirty regions, and elaborate estimates were made of the additional cost of living in a dirty region. The study separated hard economic costs from soft social costs. Among the hard economic costs were estimates of the additional money spent on detergents, laundry, cleaning, painting, repair of corrosion, and replacement of damaged textiles; also added in were allowances for extra health services, poorer crop yields, lower property values, and other "disamenities" of life in a dirty region. Among the social costs were estimates of the extra effort necessary for a resident of a dirty region to live up to the same standards of cleanliness and smartness as a resident of a clean region, including, for instance, the extra time spent on weekends cleaning the family car. There was an estimate, too, of the cost of inconvenience and distress that goes with respiratory disease (one of the questions considered was "How much would you be prepared to pay *not* to have bronchitis?").

The result of this analysis is important. The authors found that social costs of damage, which were no more than crude guesses about the money value to be attached to unquantified information, exceeded economic costs of damage, calculated from more or less reliable hard data, by something like 400 percent. Most people living in dirty regions did not in fact incur these social costs; they simply became reconciled to a lower standard of cleanliness. So the damage curve for air pollution, which is critically important for the advice the economist will give to the politician, is dependent largely on subjective and conjectural transformations of fragile values into money equivalents. The economist may warn the politicians about this, but it is likely to be forgotten when the money-symbols come to be incorporated into the decision equation.

A similar logic is used for cost-benefit analysis of proposals that are intended to benefit society. An excellent critique of this logic has been published under the auspices of the American Academy of Arts and Sciences.[14] It is an analysis of the plan to build a dam at Tocks Island on the upper Delaware River. Following floods in 1955, the Corps of Engineers produced in 1961 an eleven-volume project to build a dam at Tocks Island, which is a famous beauty spot. The average annual benefit of the dam, including facilities for recreation, was calculated as $29 million. The annual cost, discounted over 100 years, was calculated as $18.3 million. Therefore the gist of the economic advice was that it would be a rational choice to build the dam.

But the assumptions underlying these figures were not disclosed to the public until 1974, after years of controversy about the project. Let me tell you about four of these assumptions. First, the discount rate for the capital cost of the dam was assumed to be 3.125 percent, which was the rate authorized by Congress for public works in 1962. But by 1975 the discount rate had risen to 5.625 percent, which would have raised the annual discounted cost of the dam from $18.3 million to $27.5 million, thereby just about swallowing the expected benefits. Second, a quarter of the capital cost was earmarked for the purchase of privately owned land and for the compensation of the owners. But this estimate took no adequate account of the distress that some of the population would suffer at being uprooted and forced to rehouse themselves elsewhere. It lumped indiscriminately those who might benefit from selling the land with those who would be deeply disturbed by any threat of displacement. Third, 40 percent of the assumed benefit of the dam was to come from its use as a recreation center. The Corps of Engineers assumed that some four million visitors a year would come to the area initially, and that after ten years this number would grow to ten million. At $1.35 per visitor per day, this gives a net average annual benefit of $11.7 million. To accommodate this deluge of visitors the place was to have beaches, picnic areas, campsites, and so on. But an analysis of the plan showed that it assumed a density on the beaches of one person every 50 square feet—far higher than the density many Americans regard elsewhere as grossly overcrowded. It was a similar story with campsites: the plan assumed 58 campsites per square mile of the recreation area, compared with three per square mile in Yosemite and one per square mile in Yellowstone. Fourth, although recreation was to provide 40 percent of the dam's benefit, the capital cost included no provision for roads to the area, the cost of which were estimated to be something like $700 million (more than twice the original estimated cost of the dam). Nor was there any prediction about the secondary effects of the road services: cafés, gas stations, shops, and probably a string of residential areas along the routes.

Is the economist misleading the politician by trying to quantify the unquantifiable? Accuse him of this and he defends himself with two arguments. First, he asserts that choices (some economists would say "all choices") can be translated into money-symbols. Values provide the motives for choice, so this assertion leads to the view that values can in the last resort be expressed as money-values (a formal way of saying that every man has his price). The question "What would you pay *not* to have bronchitis?" (the economist goes on to say) is not as silly as it sounds. Most people would not barter their children or their home, and some would not barter even a well-paid job, to rid themselves of bronchitis; but they would barter *something*. So a notional price tag can be assigned to freedom from bronchitis, even if there is no question of paying the price; it is the shadow market value of what you would be prepared to forego.

A recent British example highlights this point nicely. In 1968 a commission was appointed to recommend a site for a third airport for London. The resulting huge cost-benefit analysis showed conclusively that of the two final alternatives, it would have been cheaper to the tune of some £400 million to put the airport in Buckinghamshire rather than in Essex.* A recommendation was accordingly made to build at the cheaper site, despite the fact that this would necessitate the demolition of a whole village with an ancient church. Local opinion was deeply moved. At a service in the church the rector offered up this prayer: "Behold in Thy power and mercy Thy people in this village . . . who are at this time in great distress at the threat that their houses of God, the resting places of their dead, their homes and village may all be destroyed."† The prayer was answered: the government rejected the commission's recommendation and expressed itself in favor of the more costly site. It is said—it is too soon to know the exact history of the incident—that the preservation of the village and its ancient church was the most weighty factor in the government's decision. Very well, says the economist, they have put a "shadow price" on the church and village: £400 million is what the government is prepared to pay to preserve it; all choices can be translated into money. (In the event the airport was not built at all, but that is another story.)

The economist's second line of defense is that fragile values—the uniqueness of an ancient church, the beauty of the Delaware Valley, the preservation of a rare species—must in any case be brought into the decision equation, and that therefore the more commensurate they can be made with easily quantified values the better. In physics it was a major advance to replace qualitative adjectives like "hot"

* The most weighty component of this difference in cost was derived from estimates of "users' time" in the movement of passengers and freight to and from the airport.

† Note the use of value-as-symbol: "the resting places of their dead."

51

and "cold" by the quantitative measure of temperature. Similarly, in economics, attempts should be made to replace adjectives like "healthy," "tranquil," "rare," and "beautiful" by quantitative measures, however crude. And the way to do this is to ask, What else are you prepared to forgo (or how much are you prepared to pay) to be healthy or tranquil, or to preserve this rare or beautiful thing?

This, then, is the second of the two options open to the economist who gives advice on the protection of the environment; it is the alternative to admitting that some values cannot be transformed into dollar equivalents. I think it is the wrong option, wrong not logically but morally. I do not dispute that the economist's case is logical. The act of making rational choices can subsume more than one kind of value; therefore the logic of rational choice may be valid for choices other than those confined to market value. It may be a choice guided by value-as-usefulness (as when I choose to spend some of my pension on health insurance); or guided by value-as-intrinsic worth (as when I choose to spend some of it on music); or even by value-as-symbol (as when I prefer to carry a British passport rather than one from any other country.) In all these choices it is *logical* to conjecture the material benefits I am prepared to forego in order to secure these satisfactions. My criticism of the attempt to quantify fragile values rests on grounds of morality, not logic.*

* In common usage, the words "moral" and "immoral" have overtones that are not intended in this context. I am indebted to Meredith

In order to quantify a fragile value (beauty in a land-scape, purity in a river, life in a human being), you have to simplify it. In order to simplify it you have to divest it of qualities that are the essence of the value you are quantifying, so that what you do quantify is not the value you started with, but a residue of it, drained of much of its meaning.

Think for a moment of the techniques that are used to quantify the value of a human life.[15] One technique is to assess the value as human capital, which is the person's expected productive output into the economy minus his expected consumption. This is a common basis for compensation awards in court. It relates the value of human life to age and earning capacity. Its *reductio ad absurdum* would be to cull senior citizens from time to time because their value as human capital is negative. Another technique is to use the life tables calculated by insurance companies, which reflect investment in the statistical chances of survival. Yet another technique is implicit in some decisions in social and environmental policy. It is to decide how much money can reasonably be invested to reduce the statistical probability of death in the population owing to some environmental hazard like floods, or highway fatalities, or (as happened in America in the fall of 1976) influenza.

Wilson for the suggestion that the attitude of those economists who believe that practically every value can be quantified as money value is not a question of morality (as the word is commonly used) but of *hubris* (overbearing presumption), or—a Yiddish word—*chutzpah.*

Another technique is to calculate *ex post facto* what the societal cost of a death is. (The National Highway and Traffic Administration did this recently and found that the cost of a car fatality was $200,725, including an allowance of $17,000 for what was described as "pain and suffering.") In calculations such as these the human significance of death is drained away: the finality, the grief, the emptiness afterwards. That is why I suggest that this approach to the incorporation of fragile values is morally open to question; it gives an illusion of precision to something that it would be better to confess is unquantifiable. If it were left unquantified it would not be neglected: decision-makers would simply have to incorporate it in their decisions in some other way.

To quantify fragile values not only drains them of some of their meaning; it invests them also with a false meaning. The world of the economist is a marketplace where people are assumed to act rationally out of self-interest, under constraints that optimize the satisfaction (or utility) for both the trader and the customer. It is a world where social evaluations, from the need to protect wilderness to the price to be paid for beer, are measured on a scale of consumer preferences. To bring altruism, sentiment, and empathy for nature into this world is to examine these qualities against the implicit criterion of cost-benefit analysis, namely economic efficiency. Thus—to take altruism—if you reduce it to a form of egoism, saying that to serve the interests of others unselfishly, even at the cost of your own self-interest, is only another way of satisfying your self-esteem, then you could quantify it. The logic is impeccable: we are all prepared to pay some price or to forego some benefit to preserve our self-esteem. That price is the "shadow price" of altruism. But consider how the value has been debased to get this quantification.

Disillusion with Cost-Benefit Analysis

To end this lecture I come back to my theme. The scientists' contribution to decision-making about the environment remains influential because scientists have not tried to include in their advice information that cannot be treated credibly by their techniques. What they quantify obviously lends itself to quantification. Difficulties arise when the scientists' reservations are disregarded, or when their findings are equivocal or indecisive. The current mood of society toward the protection of the environment is, if anything, to overreact to the warnings of scientists and to turn a deaf ear to their reassurances. Thus costly measures to cut down emissions of carbon monoxide from automobile exhausts are not really justified on scientific grounds, but politicians have been obliged by pressure from the public to take these measures.[16] Hasty legislation to phase out phosphates from detergents was another example of overreaction. Resistance to the siting of power stations and dams, and the campaign against the oil pipeline in Alaska, are further examples of the sensitivity of public opinion to threats against the environment.[17] A generation ago there was no such mood in America or Britain. It is one of the signs that there is a reconciliation of man with nature.

The economists' contribution to decision-making about the environment has—in contrast to the scientists'—lost some of its influence. Enthusiasm for cost-benefit analysis as an instrument in environmental policy has cooled. One reason for this, I think, is that economists—unlike scientists—have tried to include in their advice information that cannot be treated credibly by their techniques. Economists act with the best of intentions: they assume that proper weight will not be given to fragile values unless they are converted into money values and put into the decision equation. This assumption has been proved wrong: far from being overlooked by politicians, unquantified fragile values often overturn all the sophisticated cost-benefit studies of quantified data. This is not because cost-benefit analysis is an unreliable technique but because it embodies an unacceptable premise, namely that the question to be answered is "What is *efficient* for society?" rather than "What is *good* for society?" For some enterprises—industry, for instance, where the aim is to maximize efficiency—this premise may be acceptable. For the protection of the environment this premise is not acceptable because it warps the perspective of the policymaker. By all means use the most cost-effective way to achieve the end, once the end has been determined; but do not use cost-benefit analysis to determine the end.

So of the two options open to the economist who gives advice on policy for the environment—to restrict economic analysis to values that are unquestionably quantifiable, or to stretch economic analysis to cover values that have to be stripped of some of their meaning if they are to be quantified—I strongly prefer the first. This leaves to the politician the responsibility of including unquantified values in his decision equation. In the third lecture I discuss how he does this.

THREE

Subjective Components of the Chain Reaction

Harold Wilson, when he was prime minister of Great Britain, had to assure the public that his government was concerned about unemployment. In one of his speeches he said that 7 percent of the working population was unemployed; but, he went on to say, for the man who was unemployed this was an unemployment rate of 100 percent.

Here in a vivid sentence is the politician's problem when he comes to make a decision on some social issue. He gets objective facts about the issue from experts—scientists and economists. At the same time he gets subjective perceptions about the issue from the voices of the public, speaking through Parliament or Congress, at public hearings, in lobbies, and through campaigns in the media. Rarely do the facts and the perceptions correspond; rather, the politician has to bring them into a common intellectual framework in order to reconcile them into material for a decision. He faces a tangled conflict of values. I shall try in this lecture to disentangle the values.

It will help to start with an example. In an important essay, Starr, Rudman, and Whipple have given an example of how to calculate the social cost of disability through illness.[1] If you include simply the cost to society (I shall call it the cost on a *societal* value system) you can regard this as a flat rate per day, including medical care and lost wages. Suppose the rate is fixed at $50 per day. There will be a straight-line relation between cost to society and number of days off work, rising to a figure of $18,250 after a year and $100,000 after about 5.5 years (see Figure 2). If all that matters is the welfare of the state (as might be the case in a dictatorship or a military organization), then this is a rough and ready—but good enough—estimate of the value of a human life. But for the worker disabled by silicosis for five years, for his wife who nurses him, and for his children, the relation of social cost to days off work is not a straight line; it rises steeply as the family realize that father will never get back to work and that the illness is going to end in premature death. This steep line is the social cost on a *personal* value system. Its shape cannot be calculated from hard data, but it certainly does not coincide with the flat-rate cost on a societal value system. Here is the conflict of values that has to be resolved when a policy is decided for compensation owing to industrial illness.

There would, of course, be no conflict of values if the welfare of the state were paramount and the feelings of individuals could be disregarded. On a societal value system the only problem is to fix the daily rate that represents the cost to society. But in a humane democracy the social cost on a personal value system matters at least as much as the welfare of the state; to disregard it would be to outrage public opinion, which is something no politician can afford to do. Yet I doubt whether the value of life on a personal value system can be acceptably quantified.

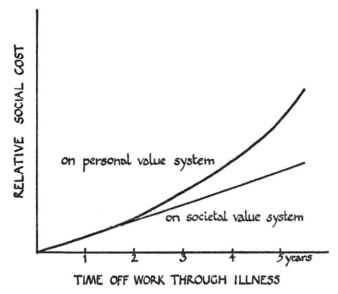

TIME OFF WORK THROUGH ILLNESS

FIGURE 2. Time off Work Through Illness. On a societal value system the social cost of disability is proportional to the total number of days of disability. On a personal value system it is assumed that the social cost of one person being disabled for a year is greater than the cost of 365 individuals each sick for one day. Source: C. Starr, R. Rudman, and C. Whipple: "Philosophical Basis for Risk Analysis," in J. M. Hollander and M. K. Simmons, eds., *Annual Review of Energy*, vol. 1 (Palo Alto, Calif., 1976), p. 637.

What is true of human life is true also of nature. Decisions to evaluate human life and decisions to evaluate the environment make similar demands upon the politician. He has to work with information blurred by uncertainties. There is uncertainty about some of the facts. There is uncertainty—indeed irrationality—about how people will perceive the facts. And there is the further uncertainty about how the politician will respond to these two kinds of uncertainty.

Assessing Public Opinion

In the last lecture I discussed uncertainty about facts. Even scientific information is not always precise; economic information is notoriously imprecise. But these uncertainties over objective advice are trivial compared with uncertainties over subjective advice; yet in democratic governments it is often subjective advice that tips the scale. How does the politician discover what people think about a hazard to the environment? And how does he assess what he discovers?

One way to discover what people think is to ask them by referendum or poll. As a way to resolve policies for the environment, this process is untrustworthy. For instance, practically everyone would vote in favor of a smoke abatement program for his community provided he did not have to pay for it. If public opinion is to be tested by willingness to pay for a smoke abatement program, then the significance of the votes will depend upon ability to pay; a "yes" from the poor should carry more conviction than a "yes" from the rich. Even with this refinement (if it were possible to introduce it) the poll would be biased in other ways. Votes could be influenced by manipulation from the media; by a fear, perhaps deliberately planted, that smoke abatement might affect employment; even by the direction of a prevailing wind that blows the smoke over some suburbs and not others.

As a guide for politicians, the simple utilitarian calculus, that the choice for society is the sum of the choices of the individuals in the society, has long been discarded. I suppose the most dramatic exposure of the hypothesis was the demonstration by Kenneth Arrow that even if only three persons vote on three choices there is no rational way to rank their preferences.* The larger and more diverse the number of individuals whose personal welfare is involved, the less rational becomes any numerical solution. The well-known "tragedy of the commons" is an example—where the welfare of the group will be destroyed if each member of the group tries to maximize his own welfare; a rational decision for each individual can result in an irrational decision for the whole group. Economic theory deals effectively with the logic of choice for individuals, but there is

---

* K. J. Arrow, *Social Choice and Individual Values* (New Haven, Conn., 1951), p. 3. The proposition is familiar to philosophers. Here is Arrow's own account of it: "Let A, B, and C be the three alternatives and 1, 2, and 3 the three individuals. Suppose individual 1 prefers A to B and B to C (and therefore A to C), individual 2 prefers B to C and C to A (and therefore B to A), and individual 3 prefers C to A and A to B (and therefore C to B). Then a majority prefer A to B and a majority prefer B to C. We may therefore say that the community prefers A to B and B to C. If the community is to be regarded as behaving rationally, we are forced to say that A is preferred to C. But in fact a majority of the community prefer C to A. So the method just outlined for passing from individual to collective tastes fails to satisfy the condition of rationality, as we ordinarily understand it."

no wholly acceptable theory for group choice. Among the reasons for this there are two simple and important ones.

First, a decision about the environment is *needed* by some people much more than by others. Improving public transport, for instance, benefits the poor more than it does the rich. In theory this spectrum of need can be taken into account by what is called the "minimax" variant of utilitarianism, whereby voting is weighted so that those most in need have the greatest influence on the decision. This is an attractive philosophical idea, but I see no reasonable way to apply it to a practical issue in environmental politics.

Second, a decision about the environment is *wanted* much more intensely by some people than by others. This intensity can be estimated very roughly if voters are asked to attach a preference value to their votes, e.g., between 5 (= I want very strongly) and 1 (= I am almost indifferent); and one might regard those whose feelings are more intense about an issue as having some sort of moral priority. But, again, I see no reasonable way to apply this to a practical issue in environmental politics. In brief, when you canvas public opinion you cannot by any trustworthy technique take account of interpersonal differences. The information from a referendum or poll may be useful politically, but this does not mean that it is an accurate assessment of public opinion on an environmental issue. Harvey Brooks recently summed up the matter very clearly: "Many affected groups may not even perceive that their interests are involved. Others may be young children, or unborn future generations. . . . People's wants and needs are not givens, but depend (among other things) on their knowledge of what is possible or available. Thus the attempts of analysts empirically to discover social goals by means of surveys . . . were doomed to inadequacy from the start."[2]

How, then, can the decision-maker assess public opinion about the environment? One way that is more trustworthy than many people think is to listen to lobbies. Lobbies are, of course, biased; they tend to filter out inconvenient information; they may create a false sense of cohesion in a group whose ideas are quite diverse; they play to win, not just to state the truth. But it is a mistake to suppose that politicians are conned by lobbies. In order to exert any influence a lobby must have a record of integrity, competence, and reasonableness. If it has these qualities it becomes a valuable source of subjective information for the politician. If there is integrity, the politician can put his tentative decision to the lobby "in confidence" and get back a reaction he can assume is that of the lobby's constituents. If there is competence, the lobby—unlike the mass of the public—can be given access to the facts and has the expertise to understand them. And if there is reasonableness, the lobby—again unlike the mass of the public—is aware of the realities of politics and the limitations they place upon political action.

There are two sorts of lobbies: those based on self-interest and those based on public interest. Self-interest lobbies are those that defend an industry against constraints that may be put upon it in the interests of the environment; and those that defend a local community against exploitation of its environment by, for example, siting a power station there or driving a highway through it. These lobbies commonly represent constituencies of people who stand to lose by the decision they are mobilized to resist. The politician knows where he stands with such lobbies, just as a judge knows where he stands with the defense lawyer in a court.

Public-interest lobbies are of a different color. Their claim to be taken seriously is that they are altruistic. Individually their supporters do not stand to gain (much, anyway) from a decision to protect the environment. They may be self-appointed guardians of birds, endangered species, or wilderness, without a mandate from any of these. So politically their case has to rest on the assumption that the public share, or at least will not challenge, their values about nature. They prescribe social values for the protection of the environment, and they have the double task of educating the public to accept these values and persuading the politician that the public has accepted the values. A lobby with a good track record gets the confidence of the public and of the government and can carry great weight. Thus in 1922, when the British government proposed to bring in a law to control smoke, the government spokesman announced: "We are awaiting the receipt of the draft Bill from the Coal Smoke Abatement Society."[3] It had been left to the lobby to frame the sort of legislation it wanted. And more recently, in the 1960's, when amenity societies challenged the highway authority on its proposals to build a motorway to bypass the town of Reading, west of London, the final route chosen was one suggested by an expert commissioned by one of the amenity societies.[4]

So the lobbies, despite the criticisms that can be leveled against them, are a valuable source of subjective information about public attitudes toward the environment; often they supply the best information the politician can get, and sometimes the information that is decisive in the making of decisions.

Public Evaluation of Risk

If this subjective information were deduced from the objective information supplied by scientists and economists, the combination of the two into material for a political decision would not be difficult. But this rarely happens. I shall digress for a few moments to illustrate this point.

A good deal is known about the risks of death from environmental and other hazards. Thus the chance of being killed by lightning is about one in a million per year of exposure. The chance of being killed in an industrial accident is about one in 30,000 per year of exposure. And the chance of being killed on the roads in Britain is about one in 8,000. When politicians have to decide about protection against floods, design of motorways, effects of drugs, safety in factories, and so on, statistics like these are an important part of the advice they get.

But there is a great gap between these statistical assessments of risk and public perception of the same risks. Take the case of road accidents. In America about 150 people a day are killed in road accidents. The news value of this carnage, and its impact on the public, are practically zero. But when some 350 people—the equivalent of 55 hours of road-toll in the U.S.—were killed in an air crash earlier this year (1977), a wave of shock went through the country and the news flashed round the world in a matter of minutes. This phenomenon is only too familiar: the public perception of a hazard is heavily weighted by its severity and very little weighted by its frequency.* It is not rational—a rational attitude would be to estimate risk by combining frequency and severity—but this is how people feel, and it is this biased attitude that dictates public opinion. That is why there is such apprehension about the risks of a major accident in a nuclear power plant. The chances of one happening (they are only intelligent speculations) are put at one in 5,000 million, which is about one-millionth of the chance of being killed in a motor accident; but this remote chance is overshadowed by the awful severity of an acci-

---

* Of course propinquity also plays an important part in public perception of a hazard; there is a sort of inverse-square law in the impact an accident has upon the public. As to the rational way to combine severity and frequency, there is a well-known legal opinion that puts the matter elegantly. In *United States et al. v. Carroll Towing Co.* 159 F 2nd 169, 2nd. Circuit, 1947, p. 173, Judge L. Hand dealt with a case of negligence against the owners of a tugboat that had caused a barge to sink. Speaking of the owners' duty to prevent a vessel breaking from her moorings, Judge Hand said: "The owner's duty . . . to provide against resulting injuries is a function of three variables: (1) the probability that she will break away; (2) the gravity of the resulting injury, if she does; (3) the burden of adequate precautions. . . . [I]f the probability be called P; the injury, L; and the burden, B; liability depends upon whether B is less than L multiplied by P."

dent if it did happen, and this irrational but very real attitude greatly affects policies for nuclear power.

So in assessing opinion about environmental hazards, the politician has to pay more attention to public perception than to statistical estimates of the risk. Indeed his job is more complicated than that, because over avoidable risks each individual draws up a sort of risk-satisfaction balance, and his *evaluation* of the risk determines his attitude to it. People accept quite alarmingly high risks, provided that they are self-imposed and especially provided that their consequences lie many years ahead. A man who would be outraged if he were exposed involuntarily to a probability of (say) one in 400 of death per year of exposure, happily smokes 25 cigarettes a day, which exposes him to just that severe level of risk. There are, therefore, some policy issues connected with the environment (smoking is one, compulsory wearing of seat belts is another) where the decision-maker needs to know not only the statistical risk but the public evaluation of the risk.

Some sort of scale of relative values attached to risks is emerging as a rule of thumb for political decisions. The mean overall risk of death per annum from disease, disregarding the effects of age, is about one in 100. The risk of death through natural disasters (floods, hurricanes, earthquakes, and the like) is about one in a million. As a very rough generalization it can be said that risks of one in a million are of no concern to the average person. Risks of one in 100,000 may elicit warnings (e.g., parents tell their

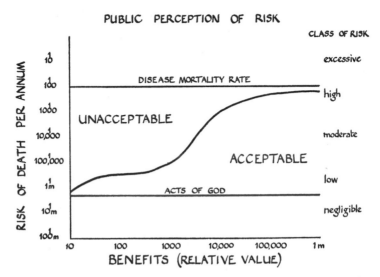

FIGURE 3. Acceptability of Risk. Schematic illustration to show the subjective relation between acceptability of a risk and the benefits derived from the risk. Source: C. Starr, R. Rudman, and C. Whipple, "Philosophical Basis of Risk Analysis, in J. M. Hollander and M. K. Simmons, eds., *Annual Review of Energy*, vol. 1 (Palo Alto, Calif., 1976), p. 630.

children not to go into deep water or to play with electrical equipment). When the risk rises to one in 10,000 the public is prepared to pay for it to be reduced (e.g., by the erection of crash barriers on highways or railings at busy city intersections). When the risk rises to one in 1,000 it becomes unacceptable to the public and there is strong pressure to have it reduced. But all these attitudes, as the diagram in Figure 3 shows, are distorted by the person's estimate of the benefits he will get from the risks.[5]

The Politician's Input

Let us now consider the part played by the decision-maker himself. At the end of this chain reaction he has to make a decision about the environment on behalf of the public.* If it involves a hazard to human health, the decision is comparatively easy. But most decisions about the environment are not so simple. They may be virtually irreversible (building a dam, adopting a fast breeder reactor); they are likely to have side effects on employment and trade; they will certainly please some people and displease others; they will contain elements of uncertainty; they will force a choice among conflicting values. It is the politician's business to manage the process of choice.

There is copious literature on decision theory under conditions of uncertainty, but most of it deals only with very simple problems, and I do not think it is of much use to those who have to make complex policy decisions. My impression is that at this stage of the chain reaction, in everything from environmental politics to the making of foreign policy, the politician relies on *hunch* (though he may dignify the process by calling it political judgment). It may be shallow hunch, as it is in the case of mere vote-catching; it may be profound hunch, which adds an input of wisdom to the other inputs I have already described.

---

* For simplicity I call him the "decision-maker." Often, of course, "he" is a committee, not an individual. But the attitudes of risk-avoidance and regret-avoidance that I go on to describe are as characteristic of committees as they are of individuals.

Decision theory will not supply wisdom to a political judgment, but it has some uses in exposing the pitfalls of hunch. Here (for example) are a couple of pitfalls.

A decision-maker's hunch about an issue depends (among other things) on two parameters: his beliefs about the issue, and his attitude to these beliefs, i.e., the weight he attaches to each of them. Data analyzed at the International Institute for Applied Systems Analysis in Vienna suggest that decision-makers cannot encompass more than between five and nine beliefs at a time about a complex issue (one example analyzed was the evaluation of a site for the disposal of nuclear waste). On such an issue as this there could be many more than nine beliefs. The decision-maker therefore has in his mind a simplified model of the issue. His response to the simplified model may well be rational, but unless the simplified model includes all beliefs critical to a decision, his response to the real issue may well be irrational. So it is important to identify the beliefs a decision-maker holds about an issue quite separately from the weight he gives to each of these beliefs. His attitude toward an issue depends, therefore, on several variables: the number of beliefs he holds about it, the subjective probability he attaches to each of these beliefs (i.e., how convinced he is that they are correct), and the evaluation or importance he attaches to each belief. Different judges of an issue give different weight to the strength of their beliefs and the importance they attach to them; and it is evident that in making holistic judgments they often do not know which cues were important in controlling their judgments.[6]

A second pitfall is that people—even experienced decision-makers—are apt, when judging probabilities, to violate the logic of rational decision-making. Thus most people, if offered a choice of $600 for sure, or a 50-percent chance (by the toss of a coin) of $1400, choose the certainty of $600. This, in the jargon of the subject, means that the utility of $600 means *more* to them than the utility of $700 (50 percent of $1400). This is a reasonable prudence; but many of these same people, if offered the choice of a 4-percent chance of getting $600 (and a 96-percent chance of getting nothing), or a 2-percent chance of getting $1400 (and a 98-percent chance of getting nothing), choose the more risky bet. This, in the jargon of the subject, means that the utility of $600 means *less* to them than the utility of $700. It is a logical irrationality; but those who make it protest that in the first case there was a certainty to balance against a probability, and in the second case only two probabilities to balance against each other. Exactly. If you make a bet on the toss of a coin or the turn of a wheel, then responsibility for the outcome is shared with the gambling mechanism. If you are unlucky, you do not have only yourself to blame: you can blame it partly on the coin or the dice or whatever. As David Kahneman has pointed out, this propensity for risk-avoidance and regret-avoidance (and for spreading the responsibility for what may be an unfortunate decision), evident in such simple operations as money wagers, raises "profound problems in the area of public decision-making."[7]

Aside from this use, decision theory applied to issues as

complex as environmental policy can do little more than monitor a decision after it has been made. What affects the decision most is the politician's attitude to environmental issues, particularly the relative weight he attaches to "hard" and "soft" values.

His options are limited, but he does have options—and that is why his input into the process matters. One option is to act as a "neutral aggregator of conflicting wants" (as Laurence Tribe put it),[8] imposing no principles upon the decision at all, and therefore no coherence upon successive decisions. This does not resolve the conflicting values; it merely sweeps them under the carpet. In the context of these lectures it presupposes that there are no principles to guide policy for the environment, only expediency; the "right" decision is the one that causes the least trouble. This is a recipe for confusion; the politician who opts for it finds himself, sooner or later, held in contempt even by those he has tried to please.

Another option for the politician is to resolve the conflicting values solely according to some dogmatic principle, which may range from personal moral commitment to party-line ideology. In the context of these lectures this presupposes that there is some fixed, immutable, transcendental goal for environmental policy that guides policy whether it has support from the public or not. I find this unacceptable: the very fact that environmental issues involve conflicts of values is a sign that the values influencing policy are not fixed and immutable. However deeply and sincerely you may believe in an environmental ethic, you cannot in a pluralistic democracy overrule public values for what you deem to be the good of the public.

The third option open to the politician is common practice in pluralistic democracies, but it is difficult to describe because at first sight it looks like a compromise between expediency and principle. In fact it is much more subtle than that. Perhaps a biological analogy will help to explain what I mean. An individual animal or plant grows according to a set program toward a set goal. Barring accidents it will reach maturity, play its part in reproduction, and die when the program is complete. Its history is determinate; its direction fixed. By contrast the evolution of a species of animal or plant does not follow any set program toward any set goal. Evolutionary history is indeterminate. All we can say about it is that it will proceed, by eliminating the unfit, in such a direction as will best adapt the survivors to their environment. But just how this will happen is unpredictable. What we do know—and it is a point essential to my argument—is that the direction of evolution is continually redefined by the process of evolution itself. Each adaptation to the environment binds the evolving organism closer to its environment. Each step in evolution forecloses some options and opens others. The process proceeds like a perpetual game of trial and error; each step is a venture into innovation, a probing into the tolerance of the environment; future steps are determined by the feedback derived from earlier steps. If you ask "To what end?," "For what purpose?," all the scientist can reply is that the only reward for biological survival is that you "stay in the game," so to

77

speak. There is no vision of New Jerusalem at the end of the evolutionary road.

Now what I want to suggest is that some social values, especially man's attitude to nature, evolve in a way analogous to the evolution of species. Analogy is deceptive, so I must not press it too far. But if you study the history of political decisions about the environment (or, for that matter, decisions about some other social issues), you find that there are no New Jerusalems at the end of their road either: goals for society are redefined by the process of choice every time a choice is made. This is notably true for the politics of environmental protection. Each political decision implants a choice into our system of social values; this imperceptibly changes the system of values, and this in turn affects the next choice.

It is a long and tortuous process. The history of smoke abatement in Britain is a good example of it.[9] In the 1840's the pioneer for smoke abatement, W. A. Mackinnon, campaigned almost single-handed for laws to oblige furnaces to "consume their own smoke." Between 1844 and 1850 six bills were introduced into Parliament. All failed to pass into law, but Mackinnon had raised a ground swell of public opinion that carried the campaign forward into the 1850's. In 1853 Palmerston did get a law on to the statute book to control industrial smoke in London. It was a very modest bit of legislation, and its initially good administration lapsed; but it did carry the chain reaction one step further. The idea that there *could* be laws to abate smoke became the starting point for the next step. In the 1880's there was a prolonged campaign, conducted by public-interest lobbies and a handful of politicians, to abate smoke more effectively, especially from domestic fires. Technologically this was becoming possible for industry through the use of well-designed steam furnaces and effective stoking; and it would have been possible for domestic fires through the use of closed stoves that burned coke or anthracite, similar to the closed wood-burning stoves used for centuries in Germany, Scandinavia, and Russia. But socially such a radical change stood no chance of acceptance at that time. To put constraints upon industry in order to abate smoke was no longer regarded as a dangerous intrusion of government into the private concerns of manufacturers. But to ask the Englishman to give up the open soft coal fire in his own home: that would have been a threat to his very liberty. The living room hearth was the focal point of Victorian family life; the fire, flickering and crackling, responding to the gentle use of a poker, was a companion to the family. Inert closed stoves, it was said, might satisfy foreigners; they would not satisfy Englishmen. So clean air remained lower in the scale of values for Englishmen than freedom to pollute the air.

But the half dozen bills for smoke abatement that were introduced into Parliament at that time, though they were withered with criticism and thrown out, did not in fact fail. They contributed to the slow ripening of public opinion; they made more familiar the notion that there *ought* to be laws against smoke. When finally, in 1956, a comprehensive Clean Air Bill was brought to Parliament and passed, the Minister was able to say that, over the terms of the Bill, there "is no difference of opinion in this House and very little outside." Some exogenous factors had influenced this change of attitude: the spread of gas for cooking, the invention of smokeless fuels that could be burned in open grates, and the introduction of central heating. There was also an economic factor: the fact that servants to clean the grate and lay the fire each morning had become a vanishing species. But the chief obstacle to smoke abatement had been psychological, not technological or economic. It took a century of persuasion for the value-as-intrinsic-worth of clean air to rise high enough in the Englishman's priorities to be embodied in law. The Clean Air Act was the culmination of a century of social evolution; when it was passed—and this is its relevance for my theme —it not only improved the air over Britain but redefined the goals for environmental policy in the 1960's and 1970's.

The art of political leadership in this process is to make proposals that are ahead, but only *just* ahead, of public opinion, and to time political action in such a way that it makes explicit what is already becoming implicit in the values held by the more articulate members of society. The password that the politician is waiting for is the word "overdue." When he hears that he knows it is becoming safe for him to act. The action he takes may be quite trivial; this is not important. The important contribution the politician can make is to ensure that the decision is incremental, that is, that it is a step in the "right" direction.

The Evolution of Values for the Environment

I enclose the word "right" in quotation marks, for it begs a question, and I now have to cross the slippery path from "is" to "ought." What *"ought"* society to do to protect the environment? I have, I hope, demonstrated that there is a trend of increased concern and that the trend cannot be attributed solely to self-interest and the convenience of human beings. But there is nothing implicitly ethical about a trend, just as there is nothing implicitly ethical about evolution.

Let me focus the question more distinctly. Has nature got a value-as-intrinsic-worth apart from its value-as-usefulness to satisfy human desires? This is a question that the politician who legislates to protect the environment has to make up his mind about. Whichever way he decides, he makes a value judgment. If he believes that nature should be respected only to the extent that man will otherwise be inconvenienced, then his yardstick for environmental policy is simply, Will it benefit society? If he rejects this view and believes that there is an intrinsic value in nature, something present in a Platonic sense even if man did not exist, then his yardstick for environmental policy may appear to some people to be a modern version of pantheism—which would hardly commend it to the legislatures of industrial societies. Agreed, that values are preferences manifested in the choices expressed by human beings; but are they no more than preferences? Or are they preferences for the *preferable*?

The question—whether nature is to be valued for its intrinsic worth—can be considered at two levels. At the level of philosophy and religion we can ask whether there ought to be an I-Thou relationship between man and nature rather than an I-It relationship.[10] I am not competent to discuss the question at this level; in any event it lies outside my theme, for it is a question that each individual decides for himself, and on this level it is not a question that a politician can decide on behalf of his constituents. But the same question can be considered at the level of science, and at this level it can offer guidance to politicians.

It is significant that the most effective defenders of nature today are not humanists; they are scientists, helped by a few social scientists. The message preached by Blake and Wordsworth is now preached (with inferior eloquence) by writers such as Dubos, Schumacher, and Thorpe. The reason is simple: some scientists have arrived (on a lower path, doubtless, than the one philosophers and theologians have used) at an I-Thou relationship with nature.

The signposts that have led them along this path are these. Scientists have become more and more impressed—awed is perhaps a better word—by the interdependence of things in nature. Animals, green plants, insects, bacteria are partners with man in the same ecosystems. No one can predict the full consequences of tinkering with any part of an ecosystem. Even the nonliving environment has properties without which life as we know it would be inconceivable. The idea of man as lord of nature is, in the minds of scientists, replaced by the idea of man in symbiosis with nature. Hamlet's comment "We fat all creatures else to fat us, and we fat ourselves for maggots" is a curt but accurate summary of man's place in the biosphere.

The technique of reductionism in science, although it has been enormously successful, does not (and cannot) illuminate the behavior of whole interdependent systems. For the analysis of complexity new techniques are being worked out: information theory, catastrophe theory, systems analysis. But these techniques cannot yet begin to deal with anything so complex as an ecosystem, and the techniques of reductionism are irrelevant for this order of complexity.* (If this seems to be an exaggeration, consider how little you could learn about the function of a computer if all you were given was a list of the components in it, together with the chemical and physical properties of the components.) Teleology (the study of purpose in organisms) was long ago excommunicated from conventional scientific enquiry, but it has left an embarrassing gap in the methodology for studying the overall behavior of complex biological systems.† You can talk about the purpose

---

* Michael Polanyi has discussed this question with characteristic insight in *The Tacit Dimension* (New York, 1967): ". . . it is impossible to represent the organizing principles of a higher level [of organization] by the laws governing its isolated particulars" (p. 36).

† One distinguished biologist who has tried to fill this gap is W. H. Thorpe in his Gifford Lectures: *Animal Nature and Human Nature* (London, 1974).

of a computer, but you are not allowed to talk about the purpose of the nitrogen cycle or about the purpose of the interdependence in an ecosystem. So ecosystems display a marvelous, but so far as we can discern a purposeless, intricacy. The enviable quality of these systems is their durability. The web of nature is not, as some sentimentalists would have us believe, fragile: it is tough, resilient, with built-in repair mechanisms. Man-made ecosystems, such as the infrastructure of cities or agricultural communities, are by contrast pathetically fragile: a power failure can paralyze New York City; an epidemic of fungi can destroy a monoculture, and (as happened in the Irish potato famine) change the course of history. Man-made ecosystems lack the stability and durability that natural systems acquire from their slow and relentless evolution. We have to live with this mystery and it has a sobering moral influence. It is no wonder that biologists who have reflected on complexity regard it as an act of vandalism to upset an ecosystem without good cause for doing so. We had better respect and preserve the stability of natural ecosystems and try to learn the secret of their stability, so that if we succeed we can apply the secret to our man-made imitations.

Considerations such as these are enough to provide the rudiments of an environmental ethic. Its premise is that respect for nature is more moral than lack of respect for nature. Its logic is to put the Teesdale Sandwort (whose destiny I discussed in the first lecture) into the same category of value as a piece of Ming porcelain; the Yosemite Valley in the same category as Chartres cathedral; a Suffolk landscape in the same category as a painting of the landscape by Constable. Its justification for preserving these and similar things is that they are unique, or irreplaceable, or simply part of the fabric of nature, just as Chartres and the painting by Constable are part of the fabric of civilization; also that we do not understand how they have acquired their durability and what all the consequences would be if we destroyed them. If you pursue this logic you realize that the view of Mr. Justice Douglas that the rights of nature should be protected through a human institution such as the law is not an atavistic retreat to pantheism. It is (I quote Harvey Brooks again) "a human construct . . . to institutionalize protection against our being carried away by temporary enthusiasms of exploitation." It has "a social function analogous to that of taboos or religious beliefs in more traditional cultures . . . a bow to the complexities we have not yet mastered and must therefore not disturb too much."[11]

In Europe and America this rudimentary ethic is already becoming incorporated into law, which is a sign that it has the consent of large numbers of people. Of course there is still much controversy; conflicts of values in environmental policy turn up again and again. But—and this is the heartening thing—people are not indifferent to these conflicts, nor do policymakers override them. The conflicts themselves are in my view immensely useful, for they provoke a continuing debate about moral choice: choice between hard and soft values, choice between indulgence in the present and consideration for the future. They oblige people

to strike a balance between counting what can be quantified and caring for what cannot be quantified. Every choice
redefines the goal for environmental policy. In the process
of choice the protection of nature is becoming more se-
curely implanted into the culture. The framework of choice
(as Tribe has put it) incorporates procedures for its own
evolution.

I have to add a tailpiece to my theme. The reconciliation
of man with the environment is a qualified success story.
But it would be false to end these lectures in a complacent
mood; for industrial societies have to make three reconciliations if they are to survive, and I have spoken only
about the easiest of the three. Two reconciliations remain to
be made. One is to come to terms with a growing scarcity of
resources: to moderate man's demands upon the earth's resources of energy and raw materials, and to determine how
affluent societies will become reconciled to a more equitable
distribution of resources. The other reconciliation that
remains to be made is the reconciliation of man with members of his own species who live by different ideologies.
Over the prospects for these two reconciliations I am not
optimistic, for two reasons. One is geopolitical: competition
for scarce resources will undoubtedly exacerbate the natural
hostility between nations with different ideologies. It will
create tensions that—if we have anything to learn from
history—tempt nations into war or international black-
mail. The other reason is, I suppose, biological. The genetic
composition of society, in America, in Europe, in the Soviet
Union, is not going to change appreciably over the next

30 years. The mounting problems of organization will have to be tackled by the same kind of men and women who are tackling them now. I do not see how these reconciliations, unlike the reconciliation of man with nature, can be made within the present political frameworks of either industrial capitalism or industrial socialism.

If my story has a moral, it is this. One of these three reconciliations is being made, not by heroic long-term megadecisions, but by the cumulative effect of wise medium-term microdecisions, each decision clarifying the shape of the decision that needs to follow. Is there hope that the other reconciliations could be made in a similar way, with a minimum of social convulsion (there will have to be some) and of surrender of personal freedom (there will have to be some of that, too)? I don't know. If we fail to make the reconciliations this way, an Englishman, Thomas Hobbes, warned us just over 300 years ago what would happen: Leviathan, the world's superstar dictator, will take charge.

NOTES

NOTES

LECTURE ONE

1. Paul Valery, *Reflections on the World Today* (New York, 1948), p. 16. Quoted by Daniel Bell, *The Coming of the Post-Industrial Society* (New York, 1976), p. 345.

2. E. T. Hall, *The Silent Language* (New York, 1959), p. 79.

3. Quoted by René Dubos, *So Human an Animal* (New York, 1968), p. 200.

4. Quoted by John Passmore, *Man's Responsibility for Nature* (London, 1974), p. 14.

5. *Environmental Quality: The Sixth Annual Report of the Council on Environmental Quality* (Washington, D.C., 1975), p. 527.

6. D. R. Kelly, K. R. Stunkel, and R. W. Wescott, *The Economic Superpowers and the Environment* (San Francisco, 1976), pp. 241, 260.

7. *Environmental Quality*, p. 376.

8. Royal Commission on Environmental Pollution, *First Report* (Cmnd 4585, London, 1971); *Fourth Report* (Cmnd 5780, London, 1974).

9. This episode is taken from Roy Gregory: *The Price of Amenity* (London, 1971), pp. 133–202.

10. A. Hill and M. McCloskey, "Mineral King: Wilderness Versus Mass Recreation in the Sierra," in J. Harte and R. H. Socolow, eds., *Patient Earth* (New York, 1971), p. 165.

11. Supreme Court of the United States No. 70–34, *Sierra Club v. Rogers C. B. Morton*, April 19, 1972, dissenting opinion of Mr. Justice Douglas.

12. C. D. Stone, *Should Trees Have Standing?* (Los Altos, Calif., 1974). This edition contains also the judgment of the Supreme Court quoted in note 11.

13. Quoted in the *Official Journal of the European Communities*,

16, No. C 112, December 20, 1973. This issue contains a 53-page Declaration of the Council of the European Communities on the program of action to be undertaken by member states, following the guidelines set out by the heads of state at their meeting in October 1972. The Council is the decision-making body for the Community. Accordingly, its Declaration has become the blueprint for the directives to member states that are drafted by the Commission of the European Communities, which is the Community's civil service. The Council spelled out in detail the principles of an environmental policy for Europe. The principles include "concern for protection of the environment and for the improvement of the quality of life at the lowest cost to the community." Action to translate these principles into practice was specified. Essentially it was to "harmonize" (a word that has led to a great deal of controversy in the Community) techniques for monitoring the environment, quality standards for air and water, effluent or emission standards for the discharge of wastes, from the north of Scotland to the tip of Sicily. There followed a stream of draft directives from the Commission. Some of these (e.g., a directive for the quality of drinking water) are for the benefit of man; but there are others whose sole purpose is to benefit nature. Thus Directive R/2005/76 is a proposal on quality requirements for waters capable of supporting freshwater fish. The explanatory memorandum to the directive makes it clear that the proposals refer only to waters where fish already live, and that the directive is for the sake of the fish, not for the sake of fishermen or people who eat fish. Similarly Directive R/2641/76 is a proposal for water standards for shellfish. Its purpose "is to encourage the increase of the shellfish population." It, too, is clearly for the sake of the shellfish, not for those who trade in shellfish or eat them. Some of the complications that arise when attempts are made to harmonize ecological conditions over the whole area covered by the European Communities were described in a debate on these two directives in the House of Lords, reported in *Hansard*, Vol. 384, No. 82, June 28, 1977, columns 1064–1105.

14. *Conservation of Wild Creatures and Wild Plants Act*, 1975, ch. 48.

15. The history of antismoke legislation in Britain is referred to again in lecture III. The story has been told, with full references to original sources, in E. Ashby and M. Anderson, "Studies in the Politics of Environmental Protection: The Historical Roots of the British Clean Air Act 1956," *Interdisciplinary Science Reviews*, 1 (1976), p. 279; 2 (1977), pp. 9 and 190.

16. Dubos, *So Human an Animal*, p. 5.

17. E. F. Schumacher, *Small Is Beautiful* (London, 1973), p. 68.

18. D. H. Meadows et al., *The Limits to Growth* (New York, 1972), p. 182.

19. P. R. Ehrlich and A. H. Ehrlich, *Population, Resources, Environment* (San Francisco, 1972), p. 2.

20. *Science*, 192, April 16, 1976, p. 240.

21. World Health Organization, *Health Hazards of the Human Environment* (Geneva, 1972), p. 210.

22. M. J. Molina and F. S. Rowland, "Stratospheric Sink for Chlorofluoromethanes . . . ," *Nature*, 249, June 28, 1974, p. 810.

23. Massachusetts Institute of Technology, *Man's Impact on the Global Environment: Report of the Study of Critical Environmental Problems* (Cambridge, Mass., 1970).

24. "A Blueprint for Survival," *The Ecologist*, 2 (1) (London, 1972).

25. Ministry of Housing and Local Government, *Report of the Technical Committee on the Disposal of Solid Toxic Wastes* (London, 1970).

26. Royal Commission on Environmental Pollution, *First Report* (Cmnd 4585, London, 1971).

27. *Ibid., Second Report* (Cmnd 4894, London, 1972).

28. N. Newsome, "Government Forced to Act on Toxic Wastes," *Conservation*, No. 40, March 1972, pp. 1–5. There is also a good but unpublished account by C. Seviour in Working Paper No. 9 prepared for a Seminar on Human Response to Man-Made Environmental Hazards, held at Indianapolis, Indiana, in 1973, and organized by the Scientific Committee on Problems of the Environment (SCOPE) under the auspices of the International Council of Scientific Unions (ICSU). The headquarters of ICSU are in Paris.

29. *The Times,* March 7, 1972.
30. A. N. Whitehead, *Adventures of Ideas* (Cambridge, Eng., 1933), p. 313.

LECTURE TWO

1. John Passmore, *Man's Responsibility for Nature* (London, 1974).
2. Department of the Environment, *Chlorofluorocarbons and Their Effect on Stratospheric Ozone. Pollution Paper No. 5* (London, 1976), p. 6.
3. F. S. Rowland and M. J. Molina, "Chlorofluoromethanes in the Environment," *Rev. of Geophysics and Space Physics,* 13 (1975), p. 1.
4. *Report of Federal Task Force on Inadvertent Modification of the Stratosphere (IMOS)* (Washington, D.C., 1975).
5. National Research Council, *Halocarbons: Environmental Effects of Chlorofluoromethane Release* (Washington, D.C., 1976).
6. *Chlorofluorocarbons and Their Effect* . . . .
7. *Report of Federal Task Force,* pp. 1–7.
8. A. B. Pittock, "Evaluating the Risk to Society from the SST," *Search,* 3 (1972), p. 285. The chain reaction between disclosure that chlorofluorocarbons (CFCs) might deplete ozone in the stratosphere and political response to this hazard proceeded very fast. This was owing in part to the intense interest the U.S. had taken in the ozone layer since controversy over supersonic transport began. In 1971 the Department of Transportation set up a Climatic Impact Assessment Program (CIAP) to report on the effects aircraft might have on the stratosphere. Interest was at first concentrated on the effects of oxides of nitrogen on ozone; but in 1973, research in the University of Michigan by R. J. Cicerone and R. S. Stolarski (Stolarski and Cicerone, *Canadian Journ. Chem.,* 52 (1974), p. 1582) threw suspicion on chlorine as a possible hazard. This suspicion was confirmed by M. J. Molina and F. S. Rowland ("Stratospheric Sink for Chlorofluoromethanes . . . ," *Nature,* 249, June 28, 1974, p. 810). Accordingly, the National Research Council set up a panel to assess the extent to which man-made halocarbons might inadvertently modify the stratosphere. This was in March 1975. A preliminary

94

report was issued in September 1976 (National Academy of Sciences, *Halocarbons: Effects on Stratospheric Ozone*). This was followed by the fuller report cited in note 5.

Since the publication of these reports there has been an adversary-encounter between the public-interest lobbies, which have pressed for immediate action to ban the use of CFCs in aerosol sprays (which account for about three-quarters of the total production), and self-interest lobbies, which manufacture aerosols or aerosol containers. The latter do not deny that there is a long-term possibility of hazard, but claim that the industry can safely be given time (two or three years, at any rate) to secure more facts and to find alternatives. (See *Science Update*, nos. 1–4, 1976. DuPont Company, Wilmington, Del.)

Meanwhile the EPA and the Food and Drug Administration announced in October 1976 their intention to ban nonessential uses of CFCs (this would cover most aerosols but would exclude refrigerators and air-conditioners, which account for only about 14 percent of production.) Yet scientific research has complicated, rather than clarified, the problem. It has been suggestd, for instance, that the two hazardous substances that seep into the stratosphere—oxides of nitrogen and chlorine—may combine to form a compound, chlorine nitrate, that would reduce the danger of damage to the ozone layer (R. A. Cox et al. at the Atomic Energy Research Establishment at Harwell in England). And there are certainly other sources of chlorine, including cigarettes! It has been said that the smoking of one cigarette produces a milligram of methyl chloride, another substance that may rise to the stratosphere and contribute to the hazard to the ozone layer. The main reason for caution in excess of that justified by our present understanding of the problem is the long time-lag between the upward drift of CFCs already in the atmosphere (over 8 million metric tons of them have been manufactured since 1931) and their effect (if they have one) on the chemistry of the upper atmosphere.

9. *Environmental Quality: The Second Annual Report of the Council on Environmental Quality* (Washington, D.C., 1971), p. 119.

10. Economic Commission for Europe, *Symposium on Problems*

Relating to the Environment. Proceedings. (New York, 1971), p. 281.

11. J. de V. Graaf: *Theoretical Welfare Economics* (Cambridge, Eng., 1963), p.2.

12. W. A. Weisskopf, "Economic Growth Versus Existential Balance," *Ethics*, 75 (1965). Reprinted in H. E. Daly, ed., *Toward a Steady-State Economy* (San Francisco, 1973), p. 240.

13. Dept. of Trade and Industry and UK Atomic Energy Authority: Programmes Analysis Unit. *An Economic and Technical Appraisal of Air Pollution in the United Kingdom.* (London, 1972). The authors are at great pains to impress on the reader that all sorts of assumptions have had to be made in their calculations and that their conclusions must therefore be read with caution and not taken too literally. However, there is no doubt about the significance of the data for the point I make in the text, namely, the preponderant part that social damage, estimated subjectively, plays in the assessment of total damage resulting from air pollution. A summary of one of their tables (VI, p. 207) illustrates this:

Estimated Current Marginal Damage Costs of Life in a
Polluted, as Opposed to a Clean, Area of Britain
(In millions of pounds [£] per annum)

Item	Mean economic cost	Social cost
Painting, laundry, and household goods, including car	0.5	170
Exterior cleaning of buildings, window and office cleaning	5.0	1.5
Corrosion, etc. of metal structures	10	–
Damage to textiles, etc.	33	–
Agricultural production	39	–
Health	40	140
Amenity	–	103
TOTALS	127.5	414.5

14. L. H. Tribe, C. S. Schelling, and J. Voss, *When Values Conflict* (Cambridge, Mass., 1976; Published for the American Academy of Arts and Sciences). See also H. A. Feivson, F. W. Sinden, and R. H. Socolow, *Boundaries of Analysis* (Cambridge, Mass., 1976; Published for the American Academy of Arts and Sciences).

15. The best recent summary of views on this topic is to be found in a research report from the International Institute for Applied Systems Analysis (IIASA) in Vienna: J. Linnerooth, *The Evaluation of Life Saving* (Laxenburg, Austria, 1975). The essay has a good bibliography.

16. Some 230 million metric tons of carbon monoxide are emitted into the atmosphere each year. About three-quarters of this comes from the burning of gasoline, as shown by the following tabulation based on data from E. Robinson and R. C. Robbins, "Gaseous Atmospheric Pollutants from Urban and Natural Sources," in S. F. Singer, ed., *Global Effects of Environmental Pollution* (Dordrecht, Holland, 1970), p. 50:

Source	Emission of carbon monoxide (millions of metric tons per year)
Gasoline	193
Coal	12
Wood (fuel)	16
Incineration	25
Forest fires	11
TOTAL	257

Carbon monoxide is a notorious poison. It combines with hemoglobin in the blood, and at concentrations of 100 parts per million (ppm) it will produce headaches and reduced mental acuity. At 300 ppm it produces vomiting and collapse. However, even in busy city streets in heavy traffic, concentrations rarely rise above 15 ppm; and the gas rapidly disperses. Thus in a street in Chicago concentrations rise to about 15 ppm during the rush hour and fall to about 6 ppm at night. If carbon monoxide remained in the atmosphere, as CFCs from aerosols do (see note 8), it would be a serious environmental problem, for the concentration would be increasing by something like 0.04 ppm per annum. The gas is stable in the atmosphere, but the background concentration has remained at about the same level (roughly 0.9 ppm) for the last 25 years. For a long time no one knew how the carbon monoxide was being removed from the air. It may react with oxides of nitrogen in the stratosphere, but the main sink is in the soil. Two microorganisms rejoicing in the names of *Methanosarcina Barkerii* and *Methanobacterium formicum* act as efficient scavengers, converting the carbon monoxide into harmless substances. These humble organisms, and a few more that have the same capacity, save the automobile industry from what would otherwise be a grave anxiety: a prospect that the global atmosphere might become poisoned from automobile exhausts. There appears to be enough capacity to scavenge carbon monoxide from the air indefinitely; and there is therefore no need to give a high priority to the elimination of this pollutant from exhaust emissions. Nevertheless, a misinformed public opinion obliges politicians to legislate against the emission of this gas from automobile exhausts, at great expense to the community.

17. Annual reports from the Council on Environmental Quality give many examples of this. Dorothy Nelkin has analyzed two case studies in a very illuminating way: *Nuclear Power and Its Critics: The Cayuga Lake Controversy* (Ithaca, N.Y., 1971); and *Jetport: The Boston Airport Controversy* (New Brunswick, N.J., 1974).

LECTURE THREE

1. C. Starr, R. Rudman, and C. Whipple, "Philosophical Basis for Risk Analysis," in J. M. Hollander and M. K. Simmons, eds., *Annual Review of Energy*, vol. 1 (Palo Alto, Calif., 1976), p. 629. Risk-benefit analysis (or as I prefer to call it risk-satisfaction analysis) was for a long time neglected; it has recently attracted a lot of attention, and rightly so, for it is often the critical input in a political decision. The dilemmas arising from the energy crisis have given a sharp stimulus to a rigorous study of risk-satisfaction problems. A decision has to be made between the risks that would accompany the proliferation of nuclear power plants, and the quite different (but no less frightening) risks of life in an energy-starved society: the choice between (in its extreme form) a plutonium economy and a low-kilowatt economy. Among the illuminating studies of risk

that have been prompted by this situation are *Perspectives on Benefit-Risk Decision Making*, the report of a colloquium conducted under the auspices of the National Academy of Engineering in 1971 (National Academy of Engineering, Washington, D.C., 1972); a series of research reports from the International Institute for Applied Systems Analysis (IIASA), e.g., H. J. Otway, *Risk Assessment and Societal Choices* (Laxenburg, Austria, 1975); H. J. Otway, P. D. Pahner, and J. Linnerooth, *Social Values in Risk Acceptance* (Laxenburg, Austria, 1975); H. J. Otway and J. J. Cohen, *Revealed Preferences: Comments on the Starr Benefit-Risk Relationships* (Laxenburg, Austria, 1975). W. W. Lowrance has written a popular account of the subject: *Of Acceptable Risk* (Los Altos, Calif., 1976). Another popular summary of the issues is in a report from a working party sponsored by the Council for Science and Society in Britain: *The Acceptability of Risks* (London, 1977).

2. H. Brooks, "Environmental Decision Making: Analysis and Values," in L. H. Tribe et al., *When Values Conflict* (Cambridge, Mass., 1976), p. 133.

3. E. Ashby and M. Anderson, "Studies in the Politics of Environmental Protection: The Historical Roots of the Clean Air Act 1956, III. The Ripening of Public Opinion," *Interdisciplinary Science Reviews*, 2 (1977), p. 190. There is an excellent study of the lobby system in Britain (it differs in many ways from the lobby systems in the U.S.) in S. E. Finer, *Anonymous Empire* (London, 1966).

4. Roy Gregory, "The M4 in Berkshire," in H. Kimber and J. J. Richardson, eds., *Campaigning for the Environment* (London, 1974).

5. The diagram is based on data from Starr et al., "Philosophical Basis for Risk Analysis." There are good discussions of the topic in R. W. Kates, ed., *Risk Assessment of Environmental Hazards* (International Council of Scientific Unions, [ICSU], Scientific Committee on Problems of the Environment [SCOPE], Report No. 8, Paris, 1976); and in J. C. Chicken: *Hazard Control Policy in Britain* (London, 1975). See also E. Ashby, "Protection of the Environment: The Human Dimension," *Proc. Roy. Soc. Med.*, 69 (1976), p. 721.

6. This argument has been developed by H. J. Otway in *The Status of Risk Assessment,* a paper presented at the 10th International TNO Conference held in Rotterdam in 1977; and in a paper by H. J. Otway and W. Edwards, *Application of a Simple Multiattribute Rating Technique to Evaluation of Nuclear Waste Disposal Sites* (ILASA, RM–77–31, Laxenburg, Austria, 1977). See also references in note 1.

7. There is a copious literature on the psychology of choice under conditions of uncertainty, though it has not been applied to the study of actual political decisions. A reader interested in following up this topic could do no better than to begin with the papers of D. Kahneman and A. Tversky, e.g., "On the Psychology of Prediction," *Psychological Review,* 80 (1973), p. 237; A. Tversky and D. Kahneman, "Judgement Under Uncertainty: Heuristics and Biases," *Science,* 185 (1974), p. 1124; "Value Theory: An Analysis of Choices Under Risk" (paper presented at a conference on public economics, Jerusalem, 1975; unpublished). A different approach, which includes a quantitative measure of fallibility, has been proposed by H. J. Einhorn, "Decision Errors and Fallible Judgement: Implications for Social Policy" (personal communication). See also K. R. Hammond and L. Adelman, "Science, Values, and Human Judgement," *Science,* 194 (1976), p. 389.

8. L. H. Tribe, "Ways Not to Think About Plastic Trees," in L. H. Tribe et al., *When Values Conflict.* In this essay Tribe develops the interesting thesis that decisions about the protection of the environment should not, and need not, be anthropocentric. His views have been criticized, and an alternative thesis has been proposed, by Mark Sagoff in "On Preserving the Natural Environment," *Yale Law Journal,* 84 (1974), p. 205.

9. E. Ashby and M. Anderson, "Studies in the Politics of Environmental Protection."

10. There is an illuminating discussion of this by R. A. Rappaport, "Adaptation and Maladaptation in Social Systems," in I. Hill, ed., *The Ethical Basis of Economic Freedom* (Chapel Hill, N.C., 1976), p. 39. See also M. Buber, *I and Thou* (New York, 1970).

11. H. Brooks, "Environmental Decision Making," p. 120.

INDEX